Stress, Cognition and Health

'An extremely good read which provides students with a clear introduction to the many complex issues surrounding the concept of stress. Written in an open and accessible style, it relates research to everyday issues in an engaging way.'

Marian Pitts, *Staffordshire University*

Stress, Cognition and Health examines the key issues in the psychology of stress and health, bringing together a wide range of material generally not found in a single text. It looks at how the external world makes demands upon individuals – potential causes of stress – while at the same time providing them with resources to cope with stress. It covers topics such as work and employment, families, commuting, large-scale disasters and daily hassles and considers how these impact on biological processes through effects on the immune system. Individual differences in coping are explored in terms of cognitive styles and a model to guide future research is given.

Tony Cassidy is a Senior Lecturer in Psychology at Coventry University and has published nationally and internationally in the areas of stress and health. He has extensive experience of teaching psychology to undergraduate students on a wide range of courses.

Psychology Focus

Series editor: Perry Hinton, University of Luton

The Psychology Focus series provides students with a new focus on key topic areas in psychology. It supports students taking modules in psychology, whether for a psychology degree or a combined programme, and those renewing their qualification in a related discipline. Each short book:

■ presents clear, in-depth coverage of a discrete area with many applied examples
■ assumes no prior knowledge of psychology
■ has been written by an experienced teacher
■ has chapter summaries, annotated further reading and a glossary of key terms.

Also available in this series:

Stress, Cognition and Health

- Tony Cassidy

Routledge
Taylor & Francis Group

LONDON AND NEW YORK

First published 1999 by
Routledge
2 Park Square, Milton Park,
Abingdon, Oxfordshire OX14 4RN

Simultaneously published in the USA
and Canada
by Routledge
711 Third Avenue, New York,
NY 10017, USA

First issued in hardback 2017

*Routledge is an imprint of the Taylor
& Francis Group, an informa business*

© 1999 Tony Cassidy

Typeset in Sabon and Futura by
Florence Production, Stoodleigh, Devon

*British Library Cataloguing in
Publication Data*
A catalogue record for this book is
available from the British Library

ISBN 13: 978-1-138-16686-8 (hbk)
ISBN 13: 978-0-415-15813-8 (pbk)

Publisher's Note
The publisher has gone to great lengths
to ensure the quality of this reprint but
points out that some imperfections in
the original may be apparent.

Contents

CONTENTS

List of illustrations

Figures

Series preface

The Psychology Focus series provides short, up-to-date accounts of key areas in psychology without assuming the reader's prior knowledge in the subject. Psychology is often a favoured subject area for study, since it is relevant to a wide range of disciplines such as Sociology, Education, Nursing and Business Studies. These relatively inexpensive but focused short texts combine sufficient detail for psychology specialists with sufficient clarity for non-specialists.

The series authors are academics experienced in undergraduate teaching as well as research. Each takes a topic within their area of psychological expertise and presents a short review, highlighting important themes and including both theory and research findings. Each aspect of the topic is clearly explained with supporting glossaries to elucidate technical terms.

The series has been conceived within the context of the increasing modularisation which has been developed in higher education over the last decade and fulfils the consequent need for clear, focused, topic-based course material. Instead of following one course of study, students on a modularisation programme are often able to choose modules from a wide range of disciplines to complement the modules they are required to study for a specific degree. It can no longer be assumed that students studying for a particular module will necessarily have the same background knowledge (or lack of it!) in that subject. But they will need to familiarise themselves with a particular topic rapidly since a single module in a single topic may be only 15 weeks long, with assessments arising during that period. They may have to combine eight or more modules in a single year to obtain a degree at the end of their programme of study.

One possible problem with studying a range of separate modules is that the relevance of a particular topic or the relationship between topics may not always be apparent. In the Psychology Focus series authors have drawn where possible on practical and applied examples to support the points being made so that readers can see the wider relevance of the topic under study. Also, the study of psychology is usually broken up into separate areas, such as social psychology, developmental psychology and cognitive psychology, to take three examples. Whilst the books in the Psychology Focus series will provide excellent coverage of certain key topics within these 'traditional' areas, the authors have not been constrained in their examples and explanations and may draw on material across the whole field of psychology to help explain the topic under study more fully.

Each text in the series provides the reader with a range of important material on a specific topic. They are suitably comprehensive and give a clear account of the important issues involved. The authors analyse and interpret the material as well as present an up-to-date and detailed review of key work. Recent references are provided along with suggested further reading to allow readers to investigate the topic in more depth. It is hoped, therefore, that after following the informative review of a key topic in a Psychology Focus text, readers will not only have a clear understanding of the issues in question but will be intrigued and challenged to investigate the topic further.

Chapter 1

Stress: what it is and why you should know about it

And thus the mind preyed upon the body, and disordered the system of the nerves, and they in turn increased the troubles of the mind, till by action and reaction his health was seriously impaired.

(Anne Brontë, *Agnes Grey*, 1847)

The psychology of health and illness

The epigraph from *Agnes Grey* shows that the biopsychosocial model of health and illness, which is seen as a relatively new development in the health sciences, has been part of our heritage for some time. The biopsychosocial model simply reflects the belief that biological, social and psychological factors interact in an interdependent or systemic way in maintaining health or causing illness. In fact, the link between psychology and physical health was acknowledged before Anne Brontë, and when she wrote her novel in the remote Haworth parsonage it is very likely that her ideas on health and illness were as much inspired by her reading as by her experience of life.

When Hippocrates first promoted a scientific approach to medicine and healing in the fourth century BC, his approach combined psychological and physical processes. He recommended a combination of prescribed medicines or surgery and changes in behaviour and lifestyle in order to improve health. This interdependence between the physical and the psychological is even more obvious in the work of another famous Greek physician, Galen, in the first century AD.

It was really only in the seventeenth century AD, when Descartes made the distinction between psyche and soma, mind and body, that Western medicine moved almost totally into the domain of the physical sciences. (It is important to recognise that this split between psychology and biology did not occur in Eastern medicine.) Only within such a climate could it have been seen as a discovery when Freud recognised that physical ailments, in the form of paralysis, could be caused by purely psychological processes. Yet it was to be more than half a century after Freud, and much longer still after Hippocrates or Galen, before psychological evidence reached a critical mass sufficient to inspire a major field devoted to the psychology of health, i.e. health psychology. Theory in health psychology is firmly rooted in a biopsychosocial perspective, and in the words of one prominent health psychologist, *'The central concept in health psychology is stress'* (Friedman, 1992). It is this core area of stress which is the topic of this book.

A new era for health and illness

With the decrease in infectious diseases brought about by the great discoveries in medicine across the past hundred years different causes for illness began to take priority. Today the major cause of death in the USA and the UK is heart disease, followed by cancer. In the UK heart disease currently accounts for approximately 28 per cent of all deaths while cancer accounts for approximately 22 per cent. Less than a hundred years ago these would have been ousted from the ratings by infectious diseases such as tuberculosis. Among the other top ten causes of death are accidents, cirrhosis of the liver and suicide. All of these are by and large the result of psychological factors, including behavioural pathogens (risk-increasing behaviours), lack of behavioural immunogens (health-enhancing behaviours), psychosocial stress and poor coping behaviours. While germ theory still exerts a strong influence on medical practice, the majority of health professionals are moving towards a biopsychosocial perspective, in that they are recognising that health and illness involve an interaction between biological, social and psychological factors. In fact, it is increasingly being demonstrated that these factors are interdependent in a systemic way. Clearly the biopsychosocial perspective does not conform to the formistic and mechanistic thinking which has dominated medicine for the past century, and there is often a great reluctance to dispense with this tradition. Explanations which involve either–or categories (formistic thinking) and single cause–single effect analysis (mechanistic thinking) simplify life and conform to our very human need to categorise the world. Unfortunately, over-simplification provides an unrealistic view of health and illness and is very limiting in practice. It is also interesting to note that there is current concern that some infectious diseases, such as tuberculosis, are becoming resistant to the antibiotics which had previously been thought to have more or less eradicated them, at least in developed countries. This spells out a warning to a medical system dependent on chemical interventions.

Psychological factors in health and illness

The current major causes of death in our society appear to be illnesses of living which reflect demands made upon the body through living longer and increased external demands and pressures from different lifestyles. In very simple terms, the better we care for the body we have, the longer we will have it. The physical body degenerates naturally, but the process can be enhanced by the way we live. Heart disease, for example, is much more likely if we smoke, eat a diet high in fat, allow ourselves to become physically unfit and continually allow life to cause us distress. If we are distressed we are more likely to eat more, drink more alcohol, smoke and to develop a sedentary lifestyle. In addition, we need to know what is healthy and unhealthy and to follow the advice given by medical professionals. In other words, our behaviour, as a function of how we feel and think about our world, is an important factor not only in making us ill, but ensuring that we stay ill. In the past thirty years a vast amount of evidence has accumulated which shows that:

- lifestyles are directly causally related to health and illness;
- the way we think (our cognitive appraisal) about events determines the ways we respond to them – in this context whether we develop healthy or unhealthy lifestyles;
- changes in behaviour can have demonstrable effects on health and illness; and
- our attitudes to health will determine whether we hear or listen to advice from health professionals.

Behaviour, experience, emotions, cognitions and attitudes are the core concepts in psychology, making psychology perhaps the most important factor in health and illness today. They are all factors in the stress process linking the activities of living to physical and psychological health or illness.

The growth of stress research

In a recent review of health psychology Adler and Matthews (1994: 230–1) suggest that recent developments tend to be subsumable under three main questions: first, who becomes sick and why? Second, among the sick who recovers and why? Third, how can illness be prevented or recovery be promoted?' It could be argued that the first two questions are investigated almost entirely under the remit of stress research, and the answer to the third provided substantially by the same field. In fact, stress research provides the link between social factors, psychology and biology (i.e. the biopsychosocial perspective), making an understanding of the stress process perhaps the most important aspect of health psychology research. I would argue that there are no health psychologists whose research and practice are not heavily influenced by the field of stress research. The amount of time, energy and space devoted to research on stress bears testimony to Friedman's assertion that it is health psychology's core concept. In a review of the stress literature (Cassidy, 1994) I stated that over 7,000 papers had been produced on stress in the period 1988–93, and that momentum has continued with a further

10,000 publications between 1993 and 1996. The diversity of this literature is also notable. Whereas early research in the area, from a mainly biological or behavioural perspective, was conducted on animals and the findings generalised to humans, the trend seems to have been reversed. Currently findings on stress in humans are being applied to a wide range of animals including pigs, cows and domestic pets. The importance of this diversity is the recognition of the wide range of health and illness issues which can be subsumed under the banner of stress and that it is not just a human issue but reflects the struggle shared across all living things in adapting to and coping with their environment.

The roots of stress as a concept

The term 'stress' is generally said to have come from the physical sciences in the seventeenth century, in particular the work of Robert Hooke on the design of physical structures such as bridges in terms of the pressure they could withstand. Thus stress was exerted by a load, and the effectiveness of the structure was a measure of its ability to withstand stress. However, as Lazarus (1993) points out, the term can be found as early as the fourteenth century, when it was used to mean hardship or adversity (Lumsden, 1981 cited in Lazarus, 1993). Thus it appears that stress has been part of the human discourse on health and illness for at least six hundred years, and its apparent discovery in the twentieth century was rather more of a rediscovery.

Defining stress

Researchers have tried to provide a definition of stress as a twentieth-century phenomenon, and this definition has evolved through various stages. The majority of textbooks talk about three different models of stress: the stimulus model, the response model and the transactional model. Arguably they are not concurrent models but reflect the evolution of a recognition of the complexity of the stress process as evidence was accumulated.

Stress as stimulus: demands and stressors

The stimulus model assumes that stress is something which occurs in the environment and makes a demand upon the person; for example, the stress of work. Our lives are filled with situations which impose demands upon us. Moving away from home, dealing with financial pressures, examinations and coursework deadlines are a few of the many demands faced by students. Workers have to deal with heavy workloads, conflicting demands from families and work, and so forth. In fact, what this use of the term invokes are the sources of stress, or the external demands placed upon the person, in other words stressors. Research in this perspective has focused on identifying the sources of stress in the external world (Holmes and Rahe, 1967; Brown and Harris, 1978, 1989). Arguably this perspective focused on classification, the initial stage in any scientific endeavour.

Stress as response: experiential and behavioural outcomes

The response model refers to the person's experience; for example, we say that he or she suffers from stress. When we use this approach we are inferring an abstract experience called stress from observing symptoms such as irritability, lack of energy, sleeplessness, headaches, digestive problems and so on. These inferences may be from observing these symptoms in others or ourselves. This approach really addresses the consequences of the demands, or attempts to deal with the demands. They include behavioural, emotional and physical symptoms exhibited as a consequence of particular sets of demanding life circumstances. This approach has generated a vast literature on the consequences of stress in terms of psychological and physical health (Fisher and Reason, 1988; Broome, 1989). In fact, it is difficult to find any physical or psychological illness that cannot be linked to the stress process, and this is not surprising as we shall see, given the growing acceptance of the biopsychosocial model of health and illness.

Stress as transaction: stimulus, response and much more

The more recent transactional model views stress as a transaction between the person and their environment and incorporates both stimulus and response perspectives as part of a process. In fact, it is also referred to as the process model and attempts to encapture a holistic, person-in-context perspective. It entails a much more complex view of stress than the simplistic partial focus of the stimulus and response models, and as a consequence it reflects more realistically the reality of stress in everyday life. In many ways it is the culmination of a process of research over time, and has replaced the simplistic stimulus and response models of the past.

Current acceptance of the transactional model

Theorists these days have accepted the transactional approach and it is misleading to suggest that the definitional debate is still divided across the three models. When we experience stress in our lives it will involve demands made upon us, emotional, cognitive, behavioural and physiological responses to those demands, and an outcome in terms of psychological or physiological adaptation. For example, faced with an examination we will feel anxious, we will think about how we are going to approach it, we will engage in revision (or avoidance) behaviours, we will feel physiologically aroused with sweaty palms, bodily tension, butterflies in the stomach. As a result we will either take the examination or find some way of avoiding it, leading to an adaptation to the situation. This very simplistic example shows clearly that we cannot divorce the demands made upon us from our response to the demands and the consequences of the transaction between demands and responses.

The transactional, process or person-in-context approach is not simply an identification of person variables and environmental variables in the process, but – importantly – includes the inter-action between the person and their environment based on a model of the person as active and exercising agency in the process. From this **interactionist perspective** we can view stress in terms of the fit between the person and their world and draw on a useful definition of stress provided by Levi, who says about stress that:

> the interaction between, or misfit of, environmental oppor-tunities and demands, and individual needs and abilities, and expectations, elicits reactions. When the fit is bad, when needs are not being met, or when abilities are over or undertaxed, the organism reacts with various pathogenic mechanisms. These are cognitive, emotional, behavioural, and/or physiological and under some conditions of intensity, frequency or duration, and the presence or absence of certain interacting variables, they may lead to the precursors of disease.
>
> (Levi, 1987: 24)

A critical view of stress

Lumsden (1981) identifies a current problem in the area in the title of his paper '*Is the concept of "stress" of any use anymore?*' Others have described stress as a modern myth (Briner, 1994). The issue relates to the widespread use of the term and is based on the notion that stress as a concept evolved in the recent past and has come to be used so widely that it is meaningless. Daily on television and in newspapers we see reports of stress and stress remedies. Arguably stress is not a recent concept, but what is recent is the attempts to produce evidence for it using a scientific methodology. Part of the problem originates in the confusions and discrepancies that arise in the definition of stress. Most texts talk of the three different ways in which theorists have defined stress: the stimulus model, the response model and the transac-tional model described above. The critique based on definitions no longer has credibility since the majority, if not all, stress researchers these days use the transactional model. The widespread use of the term 'stress' is also objected to on the grounds that it can be used to explain everything and as a result explains nothing. The question that is raised concerns whether we should dispense with the term altogether in research and practice, or whether it can be usefully maintained.

In defence of stress

Stress research encompasses the range of areas that apply to the process which begins with a demand or set of demands on the person, involves the person's appraisal and response to those demands and includes the behaviour and experience of the person (including both mental and physical health), as a consequence of the demands and their response to the demands. I have managed to summarise the stress process without using the term 'stress' itself. Indeed, much of what we will deal with is already well known in the literature by other terms. However, the use of the descriptor 'stress' helps to unite a disparate field which is too often treated as if it were a number of different areas rather than the systemically interdependent process which in fact it is. In reviewing the evidence we will be forced by necessity to consider different parts of the process in isolation, before we can begin to develop an integrative picture of the whole. However, the reader should be aware that this division into parts is simply a heuristic in pursuit of simplification. It makes little sense, as we shall see, to consider demands imposed upon the person by their world in isolation from the person's perception and appraisal of those demands. In addition, it is incomplete to consider the person's coping responses in isolation from the health consequences which those coping responses produce. In fact, the health consequences themselves may in turn become part of the demands imposed upon the person, demonstrating the dynamic interdependence of the process. We will return to this critique of stress in the final chapter when the reader will have gained some understanding of the current research evidence.

Summary

In this chapter we have argued that the paramount importance of psychological factors in health and illness is supported by research evidence and by developments in the health sciences. The reduction of illness and the improvement of health depend upon understanding how people appraise and cope with demands imposed upon them by their world. Researchers have increasingly recognised the crucial role played by external demands and psychological processes in health and illness, and have chosen generally to research these processes under the umbrella of stress. Initially researchers focused on either the demands themselves or on the person's response to the demands, leading to some ambiguity over definitions of stress. In the past twenty or so years the complexity of the stress process has been acknowledged by the acceptance among researchers of a transactional or process model of stress wherein demands and psychological processes are seen as parts of a complex, systemic process. Thus stress is defined in terms of the fit between the person and their world, where a lack of fit produces physical or psychological illness, or both. Arguably we could discuss, describe and research this process without using the term 'stress' but it seems that this might prolong the reductionist approach which caused much of the confusion in the first place. In this sense, the concept of stress serves to pull together a complex and multifaceted process which plays a key role in health and illness.

Overview of following chapters

In Chapter 2 we move on to explore the evolution of stress research from a predominantly biological focus on explaining emotions. The core argument is that while this biological focus has helped enormously in understanding the bodily response to stress, the relationship between stress, emotion and health or illness cannot be understood in the absence of an understanding of the psychological processes, in particular cognitions, which mediate the process.

In Chapter 3 we will explore the external environment as a source of stress through demands imposed on people. This reflects an attempt to quantify the effect of environmental demands, mainly through the categorisation of stressors. The core argument is that while categorisation is a useful aid to simplification, ultimately any event can be a stressor but will become so only in the mind of the person perceiving it. This brings us again to the central role of cognition in stress.

Chapter 4 will consider an alternative view of the external environment; that is, as a provider of resources which enhance physical and mental health. There has been a tendency to focus on the negative – to focus on what causes illness rather than on what promotes health. In this way the environment has been explored as a source of stress while its potential to enhance the individual's ability to cope has been ignored. The major resources in the environment are opportunities for power/control and social support. The core argument is that these resources are ultimately defined as such in the mind of the person, thus once again highlighting the importance of cognition in the process.

The conclusion from Chapters 3 and 4 that it is not so much the objective external environment that influences health and illness; rather, its subjective reflection in the mind of the individual leads to a focus on the person in the stress process. Chapter 5 will consider the person focus in terms of traditional personality perspectives. The core argument here is that while personality perspectives do provide evidence of particular traits which mediate the stress effect, the conception of these traits as temporally and situationally stable is neither helpful nor supported by the evidence. Rather it appears that these traits are very much subject to change over time and across situations, and can be more usefully described as cognitive styles.

Chapter 6 takes up the argument that person factors are best explained in cognitive terms. It explores alternative research from a cognitive–behavioural perspective that has provided a range of concepts which help explain the person aspect of stress more directly and effectively and which can incorporate the evidence from the personality approach. The core argument is that the person aspect of stress can best be viewed in terms of appraisal and coping processes which are reflected in cognitive styles, but that the current literature is unhelpful to the extent that it presents a number of different concepts as competing explanations when in fact they each contribute to a more complete explanation. This points to the need for an integrative model of the cognitive aspect of stress.

The discussion throughout the text reflects a person-in-context view of human behaviour and experience, with the person and their context being considered separately in order to simplify the conveyance of information to the reader, and to reflect the way the literature has traditionally been organised. Chapter 7 will try to bring the various parts together and provide an integrative model of stress. The core argument is that an integrative model based on a number of principles which are evident in the research literature can be a useful guide both to understanding the current evidence on stress and in guiding future research.

In Chapter 8 we will finish with a look at some potential future developments in the field. These future developments tend generally to radiate from current dissatisfaction with traditional reductionist and quantitative approaches. This leads to suggestions that we need to engage more effectively with understanding the meaning of stress for individuals and being more inclusive and holistic in our analysis. This seems to indicate that future work must incorporate other theoretical and methodological perspectives and explore other areas of life experience.

Further reading

Introductory chapters in most health psychology texts will provide a more detailed discussion of the historical evolution of health psychology. For a general review of psychological factors in health the following is useful:

Adler, N. and Matthews, K. (1994). Health psychology: why do some people get sick and some stay well? *Annual Review of Psychology*, 45, 229–59.

Chapter 2
_____

Biology, emotion and stress

chapter 2

The roots of modern stress research

A good place to start is with the early stirrings of the modern psychology of emotions as the age of Enlightenment spawned the scientific approach to human behaviour and experience. Descartes's ideas on determinism, developments in biological science culminating in Darwin's theory of evolution and the academic trend towards empirical study of human behaviour and experience led to a move away from treating humans as special and distinct from animals and other living organisms. It is here within the study of emotion that we find the stirrings of theory that have become part of the stress literature. Modern stress research was born from the larger field of emotion theory and, after a brief sojourn, it is to here it has begun to return. Lazarus (1993) provides the case and the direction for this return.

I have used the word 'modern' in describing the field of emotion theory because in fact there has always been a field of emotions; it can be traced back to ancient Greece. Historically, explanations for human emotions have been predominantly psychological. As Lazarus (1993) points out, Aristotle in the fourth century BC was describing emotions in modern cognitive terms. If anything has been learned from the empirical study of emotions since the Enlightenment, it is that as Aristotle and others down the ages have always accepted, emotion and cognition are interdependent processes and both are central to human behaviour and experience.

The contributions of Bernard and Cannon

It was Claude Bernard (1865/1961) who proposed that living organisms regulate their internal environment in response to changes in the external environment, yet are dependent on a supportive external environment for survival. The process of survival, according to this view, is an interaction between the external environment and the internal biological mechanisms of the organism. Bernard's view was a response to the vitalists, who argued that humans are driven by non-physical (spiritual) forces and therefore cannot be studied by reductionist methods. As such it reflects a biological determinism which was to dominate psychological theory of emotion and stress until the second half of the twentieth century. It is interesting that while Bernard's reductionist perspective has dominated the science of behaviour since and has demonstrated that a lot can be learned about human behaviour through reductionist means, we are currently recognising that the vitalists were also right. While their explanations may have been rather limited, cognitive theory shows that there is something – in terms of cognitive appraisal and meaning-giving processes – which over-rides the biological processes and makes the reductionist approach limited in the long run. However, this may not still make humans special in relation to other living organisms.

The process of regulating internal environments in response to external environments in order to ensure optimum bodily functioning was termed 'homeostasis' by Walter Cannon (1929). Cannon inspired our knowledge of the way in which the central nervous system monitors bodily function, picking up signals which indicate when any part of the body deviates from homeostatic stability. A response is then initiated by the brain, which attempts to counteract the deviation and restore homeostasis. For Cannon it was clear that the counteractive response could be in terms of autonomic or endocrine mechanisms to alter physiological processes within the body, or in terms of behavioural responses to alter the external environment. For example, if we become too hot in a room we begin to perspire (a physiological response) and we may open a window (a behavioural response).

Cannon suggested that events which provoked emotions can instigate the fight/flight response, thereby identifying the influence of psychology on biology. While he did recognise the psychological aspect of the regulation of bodily homeostasis, his approach was clearly biological. The fight/flight response provides an explanation in evolutionary biology terms. It suggests that all animals have a set of reflex responses, controlled by parts of the brain and central nervous system which are oldest in evolutionary terms, and which help them to survive. The fight/flight reflex is a response to novel stimuli or danger which sets the bodily processes required for fight or flight into action. External cues are used to determine whether the animal fights or flees.

Emotion or behaviour, chicken or egg?

The first part of the fight/flight process is the startle or orientation response. Think about what happens if someone bursts a balloon behind you. You jump (startle reaction) and you look towards the sound (an orientation reaction). While this is happening your heart rate increases, blood pressure rises and so on (physiological arousal), and you feel frightened (an emotional response). You might be tempted to ask which came first. Did you feel frightened before you jumped, looked around and felt your heart rate increase, or vice versa? Common sense tells us that we experience the emotion first, but the speed of all reactions is such that it appears as if everything occurs together. Clearly the first stage is hearing the sound, i.e. perceiving the external stimuli. But does the message generated in the central nervous system upon hearing the sound first instigate a physiological response (arousal), or does it first instigate an emotion? For two important early theories of emotion this very question was central. For William James (1884) and Carl Lange (1885), emotions follow physiological arousal: this became known as the James–Lange theory of emotion. In other words, if we see a bear the physiological reaction instigates arousal (increased heart rate, etc.) and a flight reaction (running). As a result of arousal and running we feel fear. We are afraid because we run, rather than running because we are afraid. For Walter Cannon (1932) and Phillip Bard (1932) the James–Lange theory was less than satisfactory. They argued that the emotional and behavioural response are simultaneous. We see the bear, run and feel afraid at the same time.

Cognition and emotion

The link between physiological and psychological responses to external events is undeniable, and was given another dimension in Schachter's (1971) cognitive theory of emotion. On the basis of a number of studies, including the classic Schachter and Singer (1962) study described below, Schachter argued that cognition intervenes between physiological arousal and emotion. Thus on seeing the bear we begin to become physiologically aroused; we make an interpretation of our situation (cognitive appraisal). If we are on an open mountainside with no barrier between ourselves and the bear we feel fear and begin to run at the same time. However, if we recognise that we are in a zoo and the bear is behind a secure barrier, we don't feel fear and we don't run. We may feel a range of other emotions depending on our attitude to animals being kept in a zoo. So the behavioural and emotional response depends upon a cognitive appraisal of our current situation and is influenced by our past experience.

The classic Schachter and Singer study involved administering injections of adrenaline to participants. Adrenaline causes the physiological arousal experienced in the fight/flight response. Some participants were told what to expect and therefore provided with an unambiguous explanation for their arousal, while some were not told and therefore left without an explanation. A third group were given an injection of a saline solution which would have no effect. Of those given the adrenaline, some were left to wait in a room with a confederate of the experimenters who was acting angrily, while some were left with a confederate who was clearly in a happy mood. Those who had been given adrenaline and not told what to expect reported feeling angry if they were with the angry confederate or happy if with the happy confederate. Those who knew what to expect were not influenced by either confederate. The interpretation of this was that those who felt aroused needed to find a label for that arousal and did so by attributing an emotional state. We first feel aroused and we then use our context to identify and label the accompanying emotion. Schachter's theory is sometimes referred to as the lability theory or the two-factor theory of emotion – the two factors being physiological arousal and cognitive appraisal.

Critics of Schachter's theory have generally accepted that cognitive appraisal is important but have questioned the simplistic role that Schachter outlined for it. The work of Lazarus (1991, 1993) among others has provided evidence for a more complex role for cognitive appraisal. It is now generally accepted that cognitive appraisal operates in a number of stages. As soon as an external event is detected (e.g. the bear appears) and physiological arousal commences, cognitive appraisal comes into play in deciding if in fact danger exists. Lazarus calls this primary appraisal, i.e. the recognition whether a problem exists. If danger does exist, appraisal processes play a role in choosing a response (do we run or fight?), a stage Lazarus called secondary appraisal by. At this stage we label our emotion. This simplistic overview, while sufficient for our purposes, does not do justice to the range of debate in emotion theory, debate which is still ongoing. In an excellent review Strongman (1996) discusses 150 theories of emotion. In his conclusion he suggests that Lazarus's theory is the best of what is available on the basis of its comprehensive coverage and the amount of empirical support for it. The work of Lazarus is central to the later discussion of stress in this book.

Hans Selye and the General Adaptation Syndrome

It was Hans Selye (1956) who fully developed the ideas of Bernard and Cannon into a systematic model of physiological stress. Selye was concerned with the physiological response to threats to the homeostasis of the organism, such as that imposed by severe cold, heat, infection or toxic substances. He observed that regardless of the type of threat, there were certain common factors in the physiological response. He termed the physiological response 'stress' and coined the term 'stressor' to describe the source or cause of threat.

From his work on animals he discovered that the common effects of exposure to stressors include enlargement of the adrenal cortex, reduction in size of the thymus and lymph glands and the development of stomach ulcers. The increased size of the adrenal cortex indicates excess activity in the production of adrenaline which is used in preparing the body for activity, the fight/flight response identified by Cannon. The thymus and lymph glands are important in the immune system, which protects and defends the body against disease. From these observations Selye built up a picture of what happens when an organism is exposed to threat, drawing on the groundwork that had already been well laid by Cannon. Selye described the process in terms of a three stage model which he called the General Adaptation Syndrome (GAS). In the natural environment the most adaptive response to threat is likely to be fight or flight. In order to do either effectively, the physical body must prepare. Heart rate increases, pupils dilate, digestion ceases, muscles tense as resources are focused on fighting or fleeing. The adrenal cortex goes into overdrive, increasing the body's arousal level above homeostasis. This is the first of Selye's three stages and he called it the *alarm stage*.

If the fight or flight is successful, the body is restored to homeostasis. However, repeated exposure to the stressor, which may occur because fight or flight are unsuccessful or inappropriate, means that the body continues to operate at above homeostatic arousal levels. For it to do this, extra resources are required, and these are drawn from those which are needed for normal bodily functions such as digestion and the maintenance of the immune system. This is the second stage in Selye's model and is referred to as the *resistance stage*. It may appear at this stage that the body has adapted to the threat and is coping. However, damage is being done through the depletion of resources necessary for other bodily functions.

Finally, if the threat is not removed, the body enters the third stage, the *exhaustion stage*. This is where the body is no longer able to meet the demands: organs collapse, ulcers develop and ultimately death occurs.

We can consider Selye's model in our everyday life. Consider individuals working in a job where they are continually being asked to do more work, to deal with more complex situations, and not being given any extra support or payment for it. Initially these increased demands make us angry (fight response) or perhaps make us want to leave (flight response). This is the initial alarm stage of Selye's model and is accompanied by increased heart rate, increased blood pressure and so on. An animal in its natural habitat faced with increased demands would generally either fight the source of the demands or flee, thus restoring homeostasis. However, the worker in our example has family commitments and cannot leave the job, and to fight would mean dismissal or even legal prosecution. So the beleaguered worker tries to meet the demands and endure the pressure. However, continued anger, increased heart rate, blood pressure elevation, etc. begin to take their toll. The worker becomes more irritable with colleagues and family, more forgetful, begins to suffer digestive problems, sleeplessness and headaches. This is the resistance phase of Selye's model. According to the model, the continued physiological arousal maintaining the fight/flight state is using up bodily resources needed for digestion and normal bodily function. What Selye did not consider are the psychological changes that are also occurring, in that the worker is probably beginning to drink more than is healthy, to neglect to exercise, to eat more convenience food and generally to feel unhappy and depressed. Eventually ulcers develop, or the continued elevated blood pressure leads to artery problems or some other ailment. The worker becomes too ill to work or suffers a fatal illness. This is the exhaustion stage of Selye's model. Clearly there is a physiological process underpinning continued demands upon the individual, but Selye's model does not include the changes in lifestyle, attempts to cope with the demands, the emotional response of the person and the role of external resources in the process. One might argue that ulcers could be the result of too much alcohol or a poor diet rather than the depletion of physiological resources. The initial alarm stage is clearly adaptive for animals in their natural environment. However, the continued draining of resources in order to maintain a bodily state which is not likely to lead to an effective response is clearly maladaptive. We will revisit the evolutionary view on this later.

Critiques of Selye's model

Selye's work has attracted two major criticisms. First of all, it tends to ignore the psychological element, particularly in terms of the appraisal of threat and the mediation of the stress process. In fact, there is some evidence that Selye was aware of the psychological aspects but chose to focus on the biological. While he was a medical student, some 10 years before he developed the GAS model, Selye observed that while a given illness may be distinguished by a small number of specific symptoms, there are a number of symptoms that are common to all illnesses. What is often ignored in textbook coverage of Selye's work is the fact that his observations of common symptoms in illness included psychological symptoms such as motivational deficits and emotional distress. These observations were to some extent lost in Selye's work on animals and a focus on biological processes.

A second criticism hinges on Selye's assumption that there is a common physiological response to all stressors. There is clear evidence of individual differences in responses to stress. However, this may be less a criticism of Selye's model and more a criticism of the fact that it stops short of accounting for individual differences in psychological and biological make-up and ultimately the whole issue of defining stressors. When a psychological component is added in terms of cognitive appraisal processes the model is still useful.

From Selye to psychoneuroimmunology

The biological approach to stress culminated in Selye's seminal work and shows clearly that external demand produces physiological responses which can cause physical damage or death. The drive to maintain a stable internal environment (homeostasis) is what controls the physiological response to stressors. As we shall see, this process is mediated by the psychological response. Following Selye the biological study of stress began to focus on a more detailed analysis of the physiological processes and developed into the modern field of psychoneuroimmunology.

Psychoneuroimmunology (PNI) is the 'study of the interrelations between the central nervous system and the immune system' (Cohen and Herbert, 1996: 114). The immune system is the body's defence against invasion by micro-organisms, including bacteria, viruses, fungi and parasites. When the immune system is weakened we are more prone to all sorts of illnesses, and a central tenet of psychoneuroimmunology is that stress impacts on the immune system to weaken its function. We are susceptible to illnesses such as the common cold when our immune system is weakened. In fact, it is often observed that after a period of demanding work we tend to develop colds – for example, after exams or on holiday from work. This observation has been incorporated in some of the research to be discussed later.

Evidence is drawn from both animal and human research. Work with animals (Cohen and Herbert, 1996) has shown that

- there are physical pathways connecting the central nervous system and the immune system;
- chemically induced changes in the central nervous system lead to changes in the immune system; and
- some chemicals produced by the immune system can cross the blood–brain barrier and alter central nervous system function.

Other studies have shown that classically conditioned behaviour change in animals can alter the functioning of the immune system (Ader and Cohen, 1993). This shows that behaviour (psychology) can directly affect immune functioning (biology) by making the organism more vulnerable to illness and disease. However, it is important to recognise that it shows an interaction in that the immune system can influence the central nervous system. In stress terms, illness can in turn become a source of stress.

The evidence from psychoneuroimmunology

The field of human psychoneuroimmunology relies generally on tests of the presence and amount of antibodies in blood or saliva. Antibodies are an indication of immune function. Effects of immune function on the central nervous system are generally assessed through effects on behaviours. Thus if we want to measure the effectiveness of someone's immune system we can take blood or saliva samples and compare the level of antibodies in it to a known healthy sample. If we want to know how a weakened immune system affects the body we look for behavioural symptoms.

Experimental studies with humans using these measures have shown that classically conditioned behaviour change can induce corresponding changes in immune function and that human performance on various tasks is affected by reduced immune function. Laboratory studies where stress is induced have produced evidence of increased **natural killer (NK) cell** and **T-helper cell** numbers and less effective cell function in the immune system generally. This immune system response can occur as soon as 5 minutes after the stress induction (Herbert et al., 1994) and can vary in duration before return to normal function from 1 hour (Kiecolt-Glaser et al., 1992) to 48 hours (Sieber et al., 1992) after the stressor has been withdrawn. This variation in terms of response of immune function to stress led to the exploration of individual differences in reactivity of immune system function and to the suggestion that there may be a disposition towards greater reactivity in some participants that makes them more vulnerable to stress (Cohen and Manuck, 1995). Recent evidence suggests that the relationship between stress and immune function is mediated by the sympathetic nervous system (Bachen et al., 1995; Benschop et al., 1994). The sympathetic nervous system is that part of the central nervous system which is central to the fight/flight response and most directly involved in the emotions.

In non-experimental naturalistic studies of stress, similar findings were produced. Students assessed during a high-stress and a low-stress period showed immune suppression during the high-stress period on a number of indicators of immune response (Glaser *et al.*, 1985, 1986, 1987, 1991). A diary study over 12 weeks showed reliable alterations in immune function as a result of variations in positive and negative life events (Stone *et al.*, 1994). Ten years after the Three Mile Island nuclear disaster, residents who had lived in the area at the time were shown to have less effective immune functioning than a control group (McKinnon *et al.*, 1989).

Immune function and affective disorder

More evidence for psychological influence on the immune system comes from studies of immune function and affective disorders. Studies show that immune function is suppressed in clinically depressed individuals and in non-clinical samples with depressed mood (Herbert and Cohen, 1993). The effect is greater in clinical samples but its existence in non-clinical groups supports the stress link. Clinical depression varies in type and severity. There are a group of depressive disorders diagnostically labelled 'endogenous depression' which appear to have a strong physiological and even genetic link. This group responds best to drug therapy, and some would argue that these disorders are not linked to external pressures and therefore do not fit within a discussion of stress. Equally there are others who would argue that all depressive disorders are related to external pressures and that it is these external pressures which cause both the depression and its physiological correlates. Whatever the stance on endogenous depression, the group of depressive disorders referred to as reactive depression are clearly linked to external events and are the outcome of the stress process. Reactive depression is seen as the extreme end of a dimension of affective disorder which finds its opposite in the depressed mood found in non-clinical samples. The argument is that the suppressed immune function found in depressed individuals is a function of stress. This is further supported by studies which show suppressed immune function to be associated with anxiety (Locke et al., 1984) and diary studies of fluctuations in mood which show a consistent relationship with alterations of immune function (Stone et al., 1987a, 1994).

Social support has also been linked to altered immune function. Individuals reporting higher levels of loneliness, divorced as against married individuals, married couples with poorer interpersonal relations, and individuals reporting lower perceived support have all been shown to have lowered immune function (Cohen and Herbert, 1996). There is some evidence that interventions using social support can have positive effects on immune function (Fawzy et al., 1993), though the area is relatively untouched by research. Social support has been shown to be an important mediator of the stress process and will be discussed more fully on p. 70. For now it is sufficient to highlight the evidence that the relationship between support and immune function is similar to the relationship between support and stress.

The relationship between denial (avoidance) coping styles and immune function interestingly yields conflicting results. Coping styles modify the effects of stress and are discussed in detail on p. 100. In a general population sample those who scored higher on repression (denial or avoidance) also had more suppressed immune function (Esterling et al., 1994), while in a sample of gay males about to be tested for HIV those scoring higher on denial had a more effective immune function (Antoni et al., 1990). In other words, those who tend generally to use avoidance as a way of dealing with problems exhibit depressed immune function, suggesting that avoidance has a negative effect. On the other hand, the sample of gay males about to be HIV tested would be experiencing high levels of stress, which should produce depressed immune function. However, those who used avoidance did not have depressed immune function, suggesting a positive effect of avoidance.

This is less confusing in terms of the literature on coping which suggests that approach–avoidance styles are separate dimensions (approach meaning to face problems head on) (Cassidy and Long, 1996) and that sometimes under high-stress conditions and for short periods avoidance may be a positive coping strategy. Following bereavement or in the aftermath of large-scale disaster denial is part of the normal coping process but it is a stage which must lead to acceptance and active coping if we are to incorporate the experience into our world and be able to move on (Hodgkinson and Stewart, 1991). Avoiding the issue gives us temporary respite from problems and allows us to muster our resources. Allowing ourselves to fully experience a traumatic event may overwhelm our abilities to cope: for example, we may be overcome by grief. However, the problems we face in our life must be dealt with at some time, and to adopt a head-in-the-sand policy with all problems is not an effective way to cope. We will discuss approach and avoidance as part of the coping process in a later chapter.

Viral challenge studies

Since the immune system defends the body against illness increased susceptibility to illness, under conditions where other factors such as changes in lifestyle are controlled should help to test the impact of stress on immune function. A number of studies using viral challenge trials (where participants are deliberately exposed to a virus under controlled conditions: for example, given the common cold) have supported the stress–immune function link (Cohen *et al.*, 1991, 1993, 1995a; Stone *et al.*, 1992). These studies involved different strains of viruses which have an effect on the upper respiratory tract (a symptom of the common cold), and clearly show that both stressful life events and perceived stress increased susceptibility to the infection. Basically they demonstrate under controlled conditions that people who are experiencing a stressful life situation and/or perceive their life to be stressful are more susceptible to viral infections such as the common cold. It is important to recognise that this susceptibility applies equally to those who are not experiencing more objective life stress than others, but who report higher levels of stress when assessed by questionnaire or interview. An appraisal of one's life as stressful is sufficient to damage immune function.

While for ethical and practical reasons most controlled experimental studies focus on the common cold, naturalistic studies have shown life stress to be predictive of herpes virus infection (Hoon et al., 1991). These studies were less controlled and therefore less conclusive, but are arguably more ecologically valid (i.e. more closely linked to real-world conditions).

Autoimmune diseases

A group of disorders called autoimmune diseases involve the immune system failing to discriminate between self and other and attacking various body systems. These include rheumatoid arthritis, lupus, types of diabetes, and multiple sclerosis. The main focus of research has been rheumatoid arthritis, and there is evidence that stressful life events are implicated both in onset and in development of the condition (Cohen and Herbert, 1996). Cognitive–behavioural interventions, which enhance the individual's coping abilities and reduce their experience of stress, have also been shown to improve the lot of those with the condition, including reduced pain, slower disease progression and improved joint condition diagnosed by rheumatologists who were blind to whether patients were treatment or control (Young, 1992). These interventions use behavioural techniques of positive and negative reinforcement on cognitions. For example, individuals are positively reinforced (rewarded) for positive thoughts and negatively reinforced for negative thoughts. One programme for rheumatoid arthritis (Bradley et al., 1987) allocated patients to one of three regimes: a cognitive–behavioural programme, a series of self-help groups, or a non-treatment control. The cognitive–behavioural programme included biofeedback training, education about rheumatoid arthritis, relaxation training, goal setting and the use of self-rewards. Biofeedback allows patients to recognise when they are becoming stressed and relaxation training enables individuals to respond to indicators of stress by making themselves relax. Combined with education about the facts (for example, that rheumatoid arthritis is not a punishment for bad behaviour) and the ability to reward oneself for positive behaviours, the cognitive–behavioural programme had dramatic effects on pain levels, inflammation of joints and physiological indicators of the disease taken from blood samples compared to the two other groups. As mentioned above, just perceiving oneself as stressed is sufficient to cause physiological change. Training individuals to perceive their world more positively and to act more positively is the basic goal of cognitive–behaviour therapies and they have been proven successful in a range of situations. Combined with changes in life situations, such as reducing the demands on the person and increasing their social support, cognitive–behavioural therapies are very effective in dealing with stress and will be explicated more fully in Chapter 7.

An area where immune function is clearly in focus is in HIV positively and AIDS, which by definition is a disorder of immune function. There are a substantial number of individual differences in the development and symptoms of HIV-related illness and AIDS, which cannot be explained by factors like poor nutrition, drug use, HIV exposure and other viral infections. This leads to a strong case that psychological factors play an important role through effects on immune functioning (Kemeny, 1994; Schneiderman et al., 1994).

For example, HIV-positive men who had recently lost an intimate partner to AIDS showed dramatic decreases in immune function (Kemeny et al., 1995). The loss of a partner can be seen to have at least three important stress-related consequences. First, there is the bereavement and its consequent grief. Second, the loss of a partner means a loss of social support and social support is an important resource in coping with stress. Third, the death of someone from an illness one has oneself increases the threat.

While negative events produce reductions in immune function, the reverse is also true. There is growing evidence that social support (Theorell et al., 1995) and stress management interventions (Antoni et al., 1991) can influence the immune functioning of HIV-infected individuals. While there are also contradictory findings, and studies have methodological problems (Cohen et al.,

1995b), taken in tandem with other evidence of psychological impact on immune function the weight of evidence supports an important effect of psychological stress on immune function. Clearly, more extensive research with improved methodology will be effective and useful in this area.

Immune function and cancer

Psychological impact through immune suppression has also been investigated in the development and progression of cancer (Anderson *et al.*, 1994). Clearly there are a great many different types of cancer, so much so that it is difficult to consider them as a homogeneous group at all. Depression has been shown to suppress immune function and there is some evidence that depression is also a factor in the aetiology of cancer (Persky *et al.*, 1987). This seems to be more related to non-clinical depression, which fits better with a stress model (Bieliauskas and Garron, 1982). Again the findings are inconsistent, which may be due to a failure among researchers to distinguish between types, severity and stage of the cancer. For example, it seems very likely that in the later stages of the disease biological damage will tend to reduce the effectiveness of psychological factors.

Two studies have shown an impact of psychological intervention. In one, immune function was enhanced in a treatment compared to a non-treatment control group over a 6-month period (Fawzy *et al.*, 1993). In the second the treatment group showed an average 18-month survival advantage over the non-treatment controls (Spiegel *et al.*, 1989).

The role of physiological arousal

Before we move on from the biological perspective on stress, it is important to identify another approach to the relationship between homeostasis and behaviour which is sometimes ignored in the stress literature. That is the work on levels of physiological arousal, adaptation and behaviour. The Yerkes–Dodson law

(Yerkes and Dodson, 1908) identifies a relationship between physiological arousal and performance which is generally accepted as the basis for a physiological explanation of anxiety. Essentially the law is based on the finding that there is an optimum level of physiological arousal in regard to performance. Levels below and above this optimum reduce performance. The effect is described as the inverted U and illustrated in Figure 1. The optimum level of arousal varies with the complexity of the task, so that for more complex tasks a lower level of arousal is best. It is suggested that arousal levels correspond to levels of anxiety, and a simple yet enduring explanation for the effect is that one needs to be a little anxious in order to be motivated but if one is over-anxious performance is impaired. For simple tasks one can tolerate higher levels of anxiety and still perform well, whereas for complex tasks anxiety begins to interfere with performance at lower levels. For example, when faced with examinations the student who lacks anxiety and is under-aroused will have little motivation to study and as a consequence is likely to do less well. Equally, the student

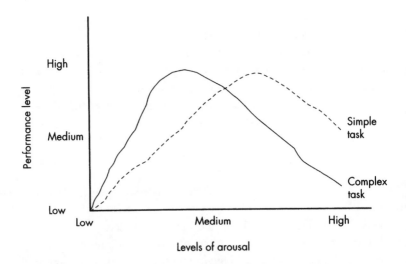

FIGURE 1 The Yerkes–Dodson Law, which reflects a curvilinear relationship between arousal and performance

who is extremely anxious and over-aroused is likely to find it difficult to concentrate on revision, will become confused and will also do less well. The best performer is likely to be the student who is anxious enough to undertake organised and structured revision, but not so anxious that their functioning is impaired. If the examination is relatively easy we can tolerate a relatively high level of anxiety and still perform well, whereas if the examination is extremely complex, any interference from anxiety is likely to have a detrimental impact on our performance.

Adaptation-level theories are an extension of arousal-level theories and simply reflect the finding that optimum levels are not necessarily stable for an individual over time. In other words, our optimum levels of arousal will change and adapt to prolonged changes in our external environment. For example, working in a noisy factory may increase our arousal level so that concentration is difficult when we first encounter the situation, but over time we adjust to the noise so that concentration is less affected. This adjustment is sometimes referred to as 'habituation'. Faced with a novel stimulus all animals and probably all living things react in one way or another. For animals with a central nervous system this reaction includes an increase in physiological arousal. However, repeated exposure to the same stimulus is met with less of an increase in arousal until eventually the stimulus elicits no observable response. I deliberately use the phrase 'no observable response' because there is evidence that change has occurred and that we may be aware of the stimulus, though not consciously so. The occurrence of a change is supported by the finding that the presence of increased stimulation leads to an increase in optimum arousal levels so that the person who moves from a rural area to the city will over time operate at a higher level of arousal, including such behavioural indices as eating faster, walking faster, talking faster and more loudly, and so on. Hence though we may have habituated to the stimulus we may have altered our internal physiological processes somewhat to accommodate it. The notion of subliminal (below conscious awareness) processing of habituated stimuli is supported by evidence that removing the stimulus leads to a response. In other words, while the stimulus continues to be present we appear not to react to it, but we will often respond to its removal. An example often quoted is the cessation of the overhead tram system in a residential part of New York City in the early 1970s. While the system operated, trams passed close to dwellings at regular intervals during the day and night. When it ceased, many people experienced difficulty sleeping, waking up at regular intervals for no apparent reason. The most obvious explanation was that they were aware of the absence of the trams. You may have experienced something like this, for example when a clock which you have been used to stops. The importance of the arousal-level theories for stress research lies in the fact that increased arousal is part of the stress response identified by Selye, and the notion of optimum levels helps to explain why the absence as well as the presence of stimulation may be stressful, as we shall see later. The importance of adaptation-level theories will become more apparent when we discuss chronic sources of stress later.

Emotion theory and stress

Although the ancient roots of emotion theory are clearly psychological, modern theory in the area since the Enlightenment has been preoccupied with the biology of emotions and developed into a biological theory of stress. The study of emotions fell out of favour in the mid-decades of the twentieth century, largely because of the predomination of behavioural approaches which had difficulty in dealing with processes that could not be directly measured or observed. Stress on the other hand could be more easily operationally defined and measured in laboratory studies. One can create situations which impose demands on individuals and measure their biological response in terms of heart rate, electrical conductivity in the skin, and the presence or absence of substances in saliva, blood or urine. Initially researchers generated stress in participants through such means as showing them a gruesome film, or setting them a difficult task. However, it was quickly recognised that stress can often be better generated in the anticipation than in the act. For example, participants expecting to watch a gruesome film will be just as stressed if not more so than if they actually watch it. This opened up a range of possibilities such as attaching electrodes and telling participants that they will receive an electric shock when no shock is ever intended. These techniques allow one to operationally define and design a stressful situation within which participants could be tested for all sorts of things. Thus the study of stress replaced the study of emotion.

The biological approach has made great strides in explaining how external demands can be translated into a physiological state within the organism. However, responses to demands in both laboratory studies and in the real world are subject to vast individual differences. In any demanding situation some individuals will exhibit symptoms of stress, but many others remain perfectly relaxed and unaffected. To explain these individual differences requires a focus on psychological processes.

Summary

In this chapter we have explored the historical development of modern stress research within the broader context of emotion theory and shown that while the predominantly biological focus of traditional approaches has been helpful, it cannot come close to a full explanation for emotions and stress without considering the major role played by psychological processes. Clearly, external demands exert an influence on the physical body through physiological mechanisms which prepare living organisms for fight or flight. In a world where fight or flight are not often viable options, the return to biological homeostasis, which may come in the aftermath of a fight or flight for an animal in the wild, is denied to the human animal. The prolonged maintenance of a fight/flight state thus depletes bodily resources and causes actual harm to the body.

A more subtle and deadly physiological response to stress comes in the form of suppressed immune function. By destroying the body's natural defences, stress leaves the person vulnerable to all sorts of infections and diseases.

Intricately interwoven with this biological response to stress are psychological and emotional processes. It is in this complex relationship between cognition and emotion that external demands are translated into stressors and the biological responses to stress are triggered. We will return to the role of cognition after we have looked at the external world and its effects.

Further reading

For a more detailed account of biological factors in stress you might want to read:

Lovallo, R. W. (1997) *Stress and health: biological and psychological interactions*. London: Sage.

For a detailed review of psychoneuroimmunology the following are useful:

Cohen, S. and Herbert, T. B. (1996). Health psychology: psychological factors and physical disease from the perspective of human psychoneuroimmunology. *Annual Review of Psychology*, 47, 113–42.

Evans, P., Clow, A. and Hucklebridge, F. (1997). Stress and the immune system. *The Psychologist*, July, 303–7.

Chapter 3

The external environment

FOR SELYE, STRESSORS WERE events that had a direct impact on the physiological organism, such as heat, cold, disease or toxic substances. However, it became clear over the succeeding years that a wide variety of events can be defined as stressors, culminating in the conclusion from Lazarus and Folkman (1984) that any event has the potential to be a stressor. Recognition of the generality of the stress process, as suggested by Selye, led a number of psychiatrists in the psychosomatic tradition to look at the relationship between life events and psychiatric disorders. The approach was predicated on the assumption that psychosocial events such as the breakup of a relationship or a bereavement could produce the same physiological response as the more direct stressors such as extreme cold or viral infection. There are at least two trends in this research: the specific, which focuses on single events or classes of events such as bereavement or unemployment; and the cumulative, which looks at the accumulated effect of a series of major life events (Holmes and Rahe, 1967; Brown and Harris, 1978).

Major life events

A great deal of research on the effects of major life events was based on the initiative by Holmes and Rahe (1967), who developed measures of life events. For Holmes and Rahe major life events were 'life change events', meaning any event which forced the person to face substantial change in their daily life and required some readjustment or behavioural adaptation. This definition included positive and negative events, something which has been substantiated in later research. Holmes and Rahe listed 43 events including death of spouse, divorce, vacation, Christmas, and minor violations of the law. Measures could be attained in one of two ways. Individuals could be asked to indicate which of these events they had experienced during a specified time period (Schedule of Recent Experiences – SRE). The alternative form (Social Readjustment Rating Scale – SRRS) had predetermined weightings attached to each event, thus allowing the calculation of a severity score. More recent scales to measure major life events include the Life Experience Survey (LES; Sarason *et al.*, 1978) and the Psychiatric Epidemiology Research Interview (PERI; Dohrenwend *et al.*, 1978). The semi-structured interview technique (Life Events and Difficulties Schedule – LEDS) used by Brown and Harris (1978, 1989) will be discussed separately on p. 42.

A large number of studies have used the Holmes and Rahe approach in both retrospective and prospective studies of life events and health. Rahe (1968) assessed the life events of 2,500 Navy officers for 6 months prior to a tour of duty and compared this with medical records during the 6-month tour of duty. The top 30 per cent in terms of severity of life events were categorised as high risk, and this group did experience significantly more illness than the rest of their comrades. Rosengren *et al.* (1991) demonstrated a significantly higher prevalence of coronary artery disease among those reporting higher levels of stress in a 12-year longitudinal study of 2,000 men.

However, other studies found no significant relationship between life events and levels of illness (Theorell *et al.*, 1975). The Multiple Risk Factors Intervention Trial (MRFIT; Hollis *et al.*, 1990), a 6-year longitudinal study of 12,000 men, found no significant link between life events and heart disease. Studies looking at the link between life events and infectious diseases tend to be more positive. Glaser *et al.* (1987) demonstrated more instances of infectious diseases among medical students during examination periods. Stone *et al.* (1987a) used a longitudinal diary design with married couples and found that there was an increase in negative events and a reduction in positive events two days before the onset of infectious diseases. Stone *et al.* (1992) tested the validity of this finding using an experimental study in which volunteers were exposed to differential levels of a virus, a design referred to as a viral challenge study (see p. 28). In an interesting viral challenge study Cohen *et al.* (1993) showed that while perceived stress and negative affect were better predictors of who became infected after exposure to the virus, life events better predicted who from those infected developed a cold.

Clearly the relationship between life events and health is not a simple linear one. The evidence is that life events and perceived stress are not the same thing and that individual differences mediate the life events–stress link.

Problems and issues in life events research

The lack of agreement across studies produced a debate in the literature during which three major criticisms were directed towards self-report measures of life events. First, there is the problem of reporting bias. It has been suggested simply that individuals who report high levels of life events may also be the type of people more likely to report illnesses, to go to their GP and generally to talk about their illnesses.

Second, there is the negative affectivity critique of self-report measures related to psychological and physical health from Watson and Pennebaker (1989). Their argument is that all these measures assess a core mood disposition which is akin to neuroticism and which they call negative affectivity. Thus any relationship between two measures would simply be a reflection of this underlying trait. Essentially what Watson and Pennebaker are arguing is that there are people who see their world in a negative light (i.e. they are high in negative affectivity). As a result they tend to feel more unhappy and discontented, and believe that they experience more negative things than people who have a more optimistic view of life (i.e. are low in negative affectivity). This leads people high in negative affectivity to respond to questionnaires by presenting themselves in a more negative way. On life events inventories they would tend to focus more on negative events and to rate events as more stressful, thus giving themselves a higher stress score. If this were the case their high stress score would not be measuring stress but rather their negative affectivity. While one can argue that perceiving oneself as more stressed is sufficient to affect health, this would still mean that life event inventories are more a measure of perceived stress than an objective measure of life events.

The third criticism suggests that measures of life events are contaminated by items which are also measures of health or illness. The obvious example is an item from the SRE, i.e. personal injury or illness. In essence, critics of the self-report approach argue that any relationship found between life events and health is an artefact of the method used. This argument relates to the definition of life events and definitions of illness. If we have an overlap between definitions, then any relationship is more likely to be a function of this overlap rather than of any cause–effect relationship. If we have symptoms of illness listed on a life events inventory, clearly people who tick these items, indicating that they have experienced more illness, will also score high on any other measure of illness. This issue can generally be resolved by ensuring that we remove items on health from the life events score before correlating the measure with measures of health.

The three critiques discussed above apply to all measures related to psychological and physical health and must be dealt with in the design and choice of measures. Ultimately they can be resolved only by using other measures such as observations, in-depth interviews or collecting information from records or peers, in order to test the validity of our results.

A further problem with the self-report measures based on Holmes and Rahe is the equivalence of events. This applies to both forms of the measure. Using the SRE, which simply considers the number of events experienced in a given period, it is clear that someone experiencing bereavement, divorce and loss of job should be treated differently from someone who has had trouble with their boss, had a change in social activities and experienced minor violations of the law. Yet both will have a score of three life events. Using weightings, as with the SRRS, assumes that any event will be of equal importance for every person. For example, pregnancy gets a weighting of 40. However, consider the woman with strong career aspirations and no desire to start a family who becomes pregnant compared to the woman who has decided she wants to be a mother. The latter is likely to view the event generally in positive terms whereas for the latter the event has obviously negative possibilities. You can apply this argument to any of the events listed; for example, Christmas is rated 12, death of a spouse is rated 100, divorce is rated 73 and change in financial state is rated 38, just ahead of death of a close friend at 37. Brown and Harris (1978, 1989) attempt to deal with this particular problem of equivalence of events in their semi-structured interview approach (LEDS).

Structured interviews and context

The approach pioneered by Brown and Harris (1978) focused on a definition of life events in terms of the emotional significance of events for the individual. In addition they preferred the use of structured interviews over self-report techniques. Interviewers received substantial training in the use of the structured interview technique developed by Brown and Harris, the Life Events and Difficulties Schedule (LEDS). As well as ascertaining the severity of the event, interviewers use probes to investigate contextual aspects of the event on twenty-eight rating scales which cover '1) basic characteristics; 2) prior experience, plans, and preparation; 3) immediate reactions; and 4) consequences and implications' (Brown, 1989: 24). Probes are follow-on questions which seek out more information in specified areas. The process is tedious and time-consuming but does accumulate substantial information about each event, therefore allowing the researcher a deeper understanding of the meaning of the event for the person.

However, in order to proceed with interviews it is first necessary to establish what is to be considered a life event of sufficient importance. From early work on schizophrenia, Brown and Birley (1968) draw up a list of forty events which are likely to produce an emotional response, and this is given to the interviewer as a guide. The forty events involve change in an activity, role, person or idea, and fall into eight groups (Brown, 1989: 22):

1 Changes in a role for the subject, such as changing a job and, for the unmarried, losing or gaining an opposite-sex friend.

2 Major changes in a role for close ties or household members, such as a husband's staying off work because of a strike.

3 Major changes in a subject's health, including hospital admissions and development of an illness expected to be serious.

4 Major changes in health for close ties or household members.

5 Residence changes or any marked change in amount of contact with close ties or household members.

6 Forecasts of change, such as being told about being rehoused.

7 Fulfilments or disappointments of a valued goal, such as being offered a house to rent at a reasonable price.

8 Other dramatic events involving either the subject (e.g. witnessing a serious accident or being stopped by the police while driving) or a close tie (e.g. learning of a brother's arrest).

It is clear that the LEDS approach includes the events listed by Holmes and Rahe (1967). In addition it considers the role of non-events, such as cases when an expected event does not occur, and the role of positive events as potential resources. In the eight categories listed above, events experienced by close ties and household members and changes in the amount of contact with others are a central theme. This reflects an implicit assumption that social support can be a source of stress or a resource for the person, and in fact in the work of Brown and Harris (1978, 1989) the role of support both from intimate relationships and within a community setting is identified as a major factor in the mediation of the stress–depression link.

Daily hassles and uplifts

Major life events are relatively infrequent in the life of any individual, yet most of us experience events in our daily lives which cause us distress. Events such as losing things, traffic congestion, being late for appointments, etc. are relatively minor in severity but their number and frequency have the potential to affect health. Kanner *et al.* (1981) labelled these 'daily hassles' and their positive counterparts 'daily uplifts', and developed a scale to measure them. Participants are asked to indicate each hassle or uplift they have experienced in a given period of time (frequency of events), and to rate the severity of the experience. Studies using the scale have shown that daily hassles are a better predictor of psychological symptoms (Kanner *et al.*, 1981) and health (DeLongis *et al.*, 1982) than major life events. However, the measures and studies are subject to the same criticisms as those for major life events.

A detailed focus on specific types of events and factors

While the research cited above focused on identifying events in an individual's life which could be defined as stressful, other researchers have accepted that certain major events such as bereavement and unemployment have widespread effects, and have singled them out for analysis.

Bereavement

Researchers focusing on bereavement have identified the process from shock, through disorganisation, denial, depression, guilt, anxiety, anger and acceptance, to resolution and reintegration, and shown that not surprisingly bereavement can have a major impact on both psychological and physical health. It is generally recognised that for all individuals short-term distress is normal following bereavement and that longer-term adjustment to the new life situation is predicated on experiencing most or all of the stages of the grieving process in no prescribed order.

One area of bereavement that has been explored by researchers is the loss of a marital partner. Epidemiological studies tend to show poorer health among individuals who have lost a marital partner, and longitudinal studies comparing maritally bereaved groups with non-bereaved confirm this (Stroebe *et al.*, 1993; Parkes, 1986). In fact, for a small but significant number marital bereavement can be life threatening (Parkes *et al.*, 1969). It appears that marital bereavement increases susceptibility to depression and to viral infection and a range of other ailments. The literature does not seem to separate out the causes of death following bereavement, but it appears to be a combination of depression, reduced immune function and changes in lifestyle leading to malnutrition. The extent of physical and psychological health consequences is mediated by factors such as the circumstances surrounding the death, gender and amount of social support following bereavement (Sanders, 1993). Individuals who have more social support and where the death is expected are less likely to suffer ill effects. In addition, males are more likely to suffer adverse consequences than females, an effect that is thought to be related to social support. There is some evidence that males in general are less effective in finding alternative sources of support and less effective in expressing their emotions than females. This can also be linked with the evidence that marriage has a more positive effect on mental health for males, probably because it provides a secure source of social support, than for females. For example, Avis *et al.* (1991) found no mortality link with loss of spouse in a US sample of women compared to age-matched controls.

Clearly it is not always the case that studies show a link between bereavement and health. Levav *et al.* (1988) found no effect of loss of a son on mortality rates of parents over a 10-year study in Israel. Again the major factor in determining consequences is the presence or absence of social support.

The role of meaning in bereavement and grief is perhaps nowhere so obvious as in the case of bereavement through disaster or war. Effects are exacerbated by the sheer number of deaths, the fact that many who die are young and in the prime of their life, death is generally unexpected, and often bodies are mutilated beyond recognition or simply never recovered. In such situations the traumatic impact is much more severe and may interfere with the grieving process which is necessary for effective coping. One important part of the grieving process is saying goodbye to the deceased. Hodgkinson and Stewart (1991) report that when hotlines are set up in the aftermath of large-scale disasters such as the Zeebrugge ferry disaster, services are inundated with calls from people checking about relatives or friends who might be involved. The numbers calling far exceed the number of people involved in the disaster, and many will be from people who have lost someone many years before and whose body was never recovered. It appears that they still live in hope of finding the person and ring up on the off chance.

This inability to come to terms with the loss in circumstances where bodies are lost was highlighted by two events in the very recent past which were widely reported in the media. The most recent hinges on the suggested identity of the unknown soldier buried in 1972 in Washington, DC. The family of the suggested person, who was shot in Vietnam in 1972 and whose body was never recovered, are seeking to have the body exhumed for possible identification. The other incident took place in the aftermath of the tragedy in Luxor, Egypt, where a number of tourists were gunned down by terrorists. The bodies of two British tourists from the same family were misidentified and the wrong bodies were sent home for burial. The extreme distress caused to the family and the efforts to find and return the right bodies attest to the human need to say goodbye to a physical body in order to be able to accept and cope with bereavement. For stress research this highlights the amount of detail required in analysing events in order to understand their effects as stressors.

Work

Stress at work is perhaps the growth industry of the past decade or so. An extensive literature has evolved on the link between particular aspects of work and health, with stress being the most widely used explanatory mechanism for people suffering ill health.

It is part of everyday conversation to talk about jobs as being on a stress continuum from high-stress to low-stress occupations. Karasek *et al.* (1988) devised a categorisation system which allows the identification of occupations along such a continuum for research purposes. Using this classification Karasek *et al.* demonstrated a significantly higher prevalence of **myocardial infarction** among men in the high-stress occupations.

Siegrist *et al.* (1990, 1992) studied male blue-collar workers in Germany and found that both self-rated stress and job-rated stress levels were predictive of risk for heart disease and stroke over a 6-year period. The effect of high-stress occupations on risk for heart disease in male workers was confirmed by studies in Finland (Haan, 1988) and Sweden (Falk *et al.*, 1992). However, a study of Hawaiian men of Japanese descent does not support the job stress–heart disease link and in fact found an opposite trend, though not a significant one (Reed *et al.*, 1989). The latter effect is attributed to cultural differences, most likely in terms of differences in coping styles.

Categorising work stressors

Researchers have attempted to identify and categorise the major sources of stress in work environments. Most commonly used is the classification developed by Cooper *et al.* (1988). From an extensive programme of research these workers suggest that sources of stress can be encompassed within a six factor model, these comprise factors intrinsic to the job, role factors, relationships at work, career development, organisational factors and the interface between home and work. The last category is often ignored or underplayed in research.

Intrinsic factors include both the content and the context of the job, and range from the quantity and quality of work, through the conditions of work to an extensive range of contextual factors such as noise, lighting and environmental design. This category provides an unending list of factors and suffers the same problems as the life events research discussed earlier in the chapter.

Role factors include such things as role conflict, role ambiguity and role responsibility, essentially all aspects of the content and performance of roles. People occupy a wide range of roles at work. For example, a manager on an accident and emergencies unit at a hospital may find conflict between trying to implement cuts in staffing imposed from higher levels and trying to support staff dealing with an increasing workload. Ambiguity may exist in terms of how much autonomy the manager can have in making on-the-spot decisions affecting emergency care. The amount of responsibility in the role is clearly extensive, ranging from responsibility for budgets to decisions affecting lives. Such a role has the potential to be a major source of stress.

Relationships involve both formal and informal relationships with colleagues, clients, subordinates and superiors in the organisation. Career development issues involve engaging in appraisal procedures, opportunities for advancement, security and competition. Organisational factors focus on a higher level of analysis and consider the culture and climate within the organisation as a potential source of stress. This includes style of management, involvement in decision-making, and group issues, and is based on the view of work organisations as dynamic open systems.

Recently theorists have begun to draw on *social representation theory* (Moscovici, 1984) and *social identity theory* (Tajfel and Turner, 1979) in addressing research and application in work experience and behaviour (Hayes, 1997). These perspectives incorporate multiple levels of analysis and explore the ways in which individuals come to have shared perceptions of the external world. Social representation theory suggests that because people interact within a shared social context they come to develop or construct shared views of the way things are. This shared view is reflected in common values, norms, in fact a common culture. This shared internal representation helps to explain the consistencies and differences in behaviour and experience. Despite vast differences in attitudes and behaviour outside work, people come to behave and to think in similar ways within the work environment.

However, the common culture may be limited to a portion of the organisation such as middle management, senior management, shop floor workers, office staff, canteen staff, etc. While there may be some very broad general values shared across the organisation there will be a set of common unwritten rules and values specific to each group which will differentiate them from any other group. Social identity theory considers the way in which the social world is reflected in categories within the mind of the individual and, combined with social representation theory, provides an effective mechanism for explaining the behaviour of work groups within an organisation. Individuals' strength of identification with particular social categories will be a prime motivator for their behaviour when particular social categories are salient. Relevant categories in the world of work might be the entire organisation, individual departments, specific work groups, and categories such as management, shop floor worker, etc.

For stress research social representations and social identity theory take us beyond the immediate context of the individual and help us understand how a wide range of higher-order factors impinge on the person. Some groups may feel excluded, undervalued and unsupported within an organisation, and this perceived lack of value may be a major source of stress. In terms of stress at work, factors at the level of the organisation or group are increasingly being investigated. This does not mean replacing the more individual-level focus; rather it incorporates all levels from individual, through group, to organisational and expands the range of potential sources of stress at work. Social identity and social representation perspectives are relatively new within psychology and are only beginning to be utilised in understanding stress at work.

The home–work interface category of work stressors is rather poorly defined but reminds us that work is only one of life's several domains. Work is part of a larger system called life and a full understanding of stress at work must incorporate the larger picture. We all know that keeping family and work life separate is impossible and that the strains of work will carry over into family life and vice versa. Yet this interaction is poorly researched. What evidence there is tends to come from a focus on other aspects such as commuting and leisure.

Commuting

Commuting is generally considered in terms of travel to and from work, but in a world where leisure is becoming increasingly important, travelling regularly over long distances is no longer simply a work-related phenomenon. There has been a massive growth in the number of people travelling over longer distances to work in the past twenty to thirty years. It is no longer unusual to find that up to 2 hours each working day is taken up with travelling to and from work. Coupled with this, rail and road links are becoming overcrowded and in many areas there is evidence of a breakdown in transport systems. Gridlock, where traffic comes to a complete standstill, is no longer a fiction. Increased levels of stress and increases in both psychological and physical illness have been found in those commuting to work both by public transport (Costa *et al.*, 1988) and by driving their own cars (Gulian *et al.*, 1989). Not surprisingly, the central factor in commuting-related stress is the degree of difficulty encountered during the journey, something that has become known as 'impedance'. Impedance is of two kinds: physical impedance, which is the actual difficulty encountered, often operationally defined as the time taken to make the journey divided by the distance travelled; and subjective impedance, which is the person's experience of how difficult the journey was. In a review, Cassidy (1992) shows that physical impedance is the best predictor of perceived stress and of health consequences of commuting. Thus it is not actual distance travelled that is important, and in fact it was shown that people who commute long distances with little impedance coped very well with commuting. For example, a person travelling from a rural area into London whose job was close to the main-line station or easily accessible within London by car was better off than someone travelling across London who had to change tube several times. It seems that the stressful effect is offset by being able to use the time to relax, read, do some work or even learn a new language. Surprisingly, car drivers tend to report lower subjective stress than those using public transport as a function of car drivers experiencing more perceived control. Part of this effect may be because car drivers feel they have more control over access to the self; that is, they are able to control their own personal space and territory (Cassidy, 1997). While the impact of commuting has been generally under-researched, what evidence is available suggests that high-impedance commuting is stressful and has negative effects on health. In addition it can have an impact on family life, engagement in leisure activities and increased absenteeism from work. It is mediated by perceived control, social support and coping styles (Cassidy, 1992).

Unemployment

In the words of the poet William Cowper (1731–1800), 'Absence of occupation is not rest; the mind quite vacant is a mind distressed.' The Greek physician Galen in about AD 200 wrote, 'employment is nature's physician, and is essential to human happiness'. These are just two examples which illustrate what has been widely acknowledged throughout human history and which logically lead us to the unsurprising conclusion that in a society which defines employment as paid work and where existence and identity depend upon the success of work, unemployment is a major source of stress. Interest in the psychological impact of unemployment tends to peak in the aftermath of large-scale economic depression and wane at other times. In the past seventy years there have been two peaks in the UK and elsewhere in Europe, the first in the 1930s and the most recent in the 1980s. Evidence from the 1930s comes from the ground-breaking work of Marie Jahoda, whose study of an Austrian village called Marienthal was published in English translation by Jahoda *et al.* (1972). From this and a further study of a Welsh mining community, Jahoda (1987) identified the stress associated with unemployment in terms of the loss of work and the functions which work fulfils for people.

A great deal of work from the 1980s confirms the negative consequences of unemployment. Studies show that unemployed people experience decreased life satisfaction (Warr, 1978), loss of self-respect and lowered self-esteem (Branthwaite and Garcia, 1985), general deterioration in mental health (Spruitt *et al.*, 1985), and poorer physical health and increased mortality rates (Warr, 1987). The effects of unemployment are not limited to the individual but affect families and whole communities (Beale and Nethercott, 1985; Orford, 1992). The effects of unemployment are mediated by social support, status in terms of financial stability and responsibilities, gender, age, labour market, local levels of unemployment and individual differences (Branthwaite and Trueman, 1989). Those with more social support, who are more financially secure, with less responsibility for family or others are less likely to suffer ill effects. Those who are just beginning their work career (younger people) and those nearing retirement age tend generally to fare better than those in between, probably because the latter have more responsibility for their family and are less financially secure. Where there are plenty of alternative jobs people are less likely to suffer psychologically or physically. However, it is also the case that where unemployment levels are high and unemployment is the norm, there is less stigma attached to being unemployed and some psychological consequences are reduced. Studies have shown males to be more severely affected by unemployment than females, but this is likely to change (or to have already changed) as more females become the breadwinners.

As you can see, the answer to the question of who is most affected by unemployment is complex. All the above factors and more, such as ethnic group, previous experience of unemployment, and so on, need to be considered. In addition, these variables do not exist in isolation. Each person will find that a number of the above factors apply to them, and those who find themselves on the negative end of quite a few will experience unemployment more negatively. For example, the father responsible for a large family who is not financially secure in an area and occupation where there is little hope of alternative employment, who lives in an area where very few people are unemployed, and who has been unemployed before is likely to experience extreme levels of stress. This may be further exacerbated if he is from an ethnic minority group.

While identifying factors that mediate the effect of unemployment is important, it is perhaps more effective to discover why unemployment has such an effect. A number of theorists have addressed this question.

Jahoda's functional approach suggests that because work provides many obvious or manifest functions such as financial security and many not so obvious or latent functions such as structuring time and social contact, the major effects of unemployment can be explained in terms of the loss of these functions. Thus she says, 'Whether one likes or hates one's job, it structures time for the day, the week, the years; it broadens the social horizon beyond family and friends; it enforces participation in collective purposes; it defines one's social status' (Jahoda, 1988: 6).

Following this lead Warr (1987) suggests nine major functions of work which can be used in explaining the effects of unemployment. These are interpersonal contract, opportunity for control, opportunity for skill use, externally generated goals, variety, environmental clarity, availability of money, physical security and valued social position. Using these functions Warr goes on to provide a coherent framework to account for the environmental demands of unemployment in terms of his *vitamin model*. He uses the analogy of the effect of vitamins on physical health. The body needs a minimum level of all vitamins for good health to exist. For some vitamins, such as C and E, an excess amount is harmless, but for others, such as A and D, an excess causes damage. Warr argues that environmental factors in terms of stress operate in a similar fashion. Some factors are necessary to a point but too much is not damaging; an example is money. Such factors have a cumulative effect in the same way as do vitamins C and E. Other factors such as variety have a negative effect in too small or too large quantities. These have an additional decrement effect like vitamins A and D. The model is illustrated in Figure 2.

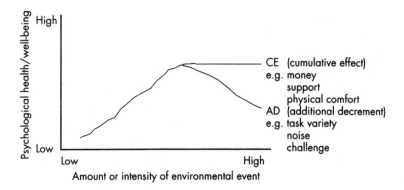

FIGURE 2 The vitamin model of the relationship between environmental events and psychological health

Source: After Warr (1987)

Warr's model focuses on the individual level and, although useful, it has been criticised for its limited focus. More recently a higher-level approach has been applied in terms of social identity theory. Social identity theory helps to incorporate a wide range of individual-level factors in a group-level perspective. In essence it suggests that our self concept includes two elements, personal and social identity. The greater part of our self concept is social and reflects how we identify ourselves as part of a society made up of a wide range of diverse social groups. We identify ourselves with a number of groups (in groups) and by default disidentify with all other groups (out groups). Consequently we compare ourselves with in-group and out-group members in ways that allow us to build a positive identity for ourselves and hence a sense of positive self-esteem. In a social world where work is important, work provides the source of much of our identity. Unemployment threatens or destroys a major part of our social identity.

Home and family

Families are probably the most important group that anyone experiences in their life and probably the single most important context for the development of psychological and physical health. Yet in comparison to areas such as work, they are under-researched in the stress field. Longitudinal research on the development of children has shown that a combination of factors such as family conflict and breakup, abuse from caregivers, poor relationships, parental mental illness or alcoholism, absence of one parent, death of a parent or sibling, poverty, crowding, time spent in care, parental criminality and the presence of handicapped siblings tend to occur more frequently in the backgrounds of children who exhibit symptoms of psychological disorder (Rutter *et al.*, 1976; Cohen and Work, 1988; Werner, 1989). It seems clear that none of these factors alone is a good predictor of stress, but a combination of several is a necessary but not sufficient condition for problems to develop (White and Woollett, 1992). It is also clear that factors such as family breakup, poverty, crowding, etc. do not in themselves indicate poor child-rearing practices. However, they do place parents at a disadvantage.

On the other hand, there is evidence that adversity may enhance coping in children. Children who have experienced different caregivers (such as baby-sitters or day care) cope better with hospital admission (Stacey *et al.*, 1970). In some recent work, individuals reporting a moderate level of conflict and high levels of expressivity and cohesion scored higher on mastery than those reporting very low levels of conflict (Cassidy and Newport, 1997). The suggestion is that experiencing life problems in the context of successful coping is a positive learning experience.

While studies show that a combination of adverse factors place children at risk for stress, only a proportion of high-risk children suffer (Werner, 1989). White and Woollett (1992: 155) suggest that factors which contribute to stress resilience in children can be categorised into three clusters: 'intrapersonal qualities such as positive personality dispositions; a supportive family environment; and access to supportive social agencies'. Broadly, the difference between children who suffer adverse effects and those who don't can be explained in terms of the type of relationships experienced at home, levels of social support and psychological factors related to the children themselves. We will look at the role of social support and personal dispositions in the stress process in later chapters in some detail. Essentially, a stressful family environment can be defined as lacking the factors that contribute to resilience, i.e. being unsupportive, and where the cognitive styles which reduce vulnerability are not nurtured. There is evidence that cohesion, encouragement in expressing emotions, and providing opportunities for autonomy and control are important aspects of low-stress family environments. It is through their effects on cohesion, control, expressivity and support that factors like parental alcohol abuse, parental separation and divorce, etc. have their impact on children's mental and physical health. However, there is room for a great deal more research on the developmental aspects of the stress process.

Cataclysmic events

A separate literature has addressed the consequences of cataclysmic events such as war or large-scale disaster for those who are directly or indirectly involved (Hodgkinson and Stewart, 1991). Studies suggest that natural disasters (such as floods, earthquakes, etc.) and human-made disasters (such as large-scale transport accidents) all share a common outcome for those involved in that a significant number will develop post-traumatic stress disorder (PTSD). However, they do differ somewhat in the severity of the stress disorder and how long it lasts, with human-made disasters tending to produce the more severe and longer-term consequences. It is likely that this is at least partly because human-made disasters are more unpredictable and therefore perceived as less controllable (Hodgkinson and Stewart, 1991). We come to expect that our trains, planes and nuclear power plants are safe in order that we can survive in a technological age. We cannot really prepare for a technological disaster in the same way that people in earthquake zones can take precautions against earthquakes. What could have been more unexpected than to be killed, seriously injured or bereaved as a consequence of a jumbo jet crashing on a small Scottish town as people slept in their beds? Yet this is what happened in Lockerbie in 1988.

As I write this in December 1997, an inquiry is under way in Russia in the aftermath of a cargo plane crashing into a block of residential flats. In addition, the traumatic stimuli (e.g. mutilated bodies) in the aftermath of human-made disasters are much more severe.

In disasters it is not just those directly involved who suffer. For example, in a large scale plane crash there will be relatives and friends of those killed or injured, the rescue personnel who work at the scene, the medical personnel who treat the injured and deal with the bereaved; the community in which the victims lived and the community within which the crash occurs will be affected and even those who watch the news coverage are potentially at risk. For example, in the aftermath of the discovery of the human remains of a number of young females who had been murdered in Gloucester, England, in what are referred to as the West murders, children living many streets away experienced nightmares and sleep disturbance.

Chronic or ambient stressors

Another distinct literature considers the effects of events that exert their effect consistently over long periods of time, even over whole lifetimes. In environmental psychology such stressors are described as ambient and include noise, weather, air pollution and other aspects of the enduring physical environment. McLean and Link (1994: 23) consider five categories of what they call chronic strains:

> a) persistent life difficulties or chronically stressful situations that can be considered corollaries of life events; b) role strain, including the strain within specific roles as well as the strain of holding multiple roles; c) chronic strains that derive from societal responses to characteristics of a person that include him or her as a class of persons, such as racism or sexism; and d) chronic community wide strains that may operate at an ecological level, such as the chronic strain of residence in a high crime area or residence near an environmental threat.

The fifth category is 'the frequency of such daily hassles as waiting too long in line or being stuck in traffic'.

This is a useful categorisation which highlights the failure in most measures of life events to distinguish between chronic and acute sources of stress. For example, many of the items on checklists may be assessing events which are long-standing demands on the individual. Chronic strains or sources of stress cut across the boundaries of the different categories discussed above. For example, role strain in terms of role conflict, overload or ambiguity can occur at work or in the home. A recent story in a British national newspaper (*Guardian*, 6 May 1998) reports that many men who try to combine work with childcare have to hide the fact that they engage in childcare from colleagues and bosses at work. If they have to take time off to pick up children from school, etc., it is better to use an excuse such as going to an important football match. Clearly they are experiencing role strain. Chronic strains pervade all life domains and remind us of the artificiality of dividing life into separate categories such as work and home.

There is evidence that both acute stressors and persistent life difficulties are related to psychological distress (Monroe and Roberts, 1990; Moos and Swindle, 1990), and in some cases persistent life difficulties explain more of the variance than acute stressors. However, it is difficult to disentangle the effects since they tend not to be measured separately in most studies. Role strain may involve lack of role clarity, too many roles or conflict between roles, and has an impact on psychological distress (Pearlin *et al.*, 1981). It appears that role strain can increase or decrease the impact of acute life events (McLean and Link, 1994). Imagine a social division and you have identified a source or target of prejudice and discrimination. People are labelled and discriminated against on the basis of age, race, religion, ability, mental status, sex, income, social background, hair colour, size and probably many other categories. Differences in mental and physical health across such categories indicate differential experiences of stress. The effect of social divisions is discussed further under social identity in Chapter 4. One of the most obvious ways in which social divisions relate to stress is through the exacerbation of effects of other sources of stress. For example, the consequences of unemployment are likely to be compounded if one is from an ethnic minority, is older and has been labelled as mentally ill.

Community-wide sources of stress, such as living in a high-crime environment, or in overcrowded conditions, are perhaps underestimated in terms of their effects on individuals (Cassidy, 1997; Halpern, 1995). This underestimation is partly due to the fact that these sources of stress are difficult to measure and therefore rather poorly researched. Crowding has been shown to be related to physical symptoms of stress (Epstein, 1982) and to increased levels of physical illness (Fuller et al., 1993). However, the best explanation for the effect of crowding is in terms of control over access to the self and involves a subjective appraisal (cognitive appraisal) of the relationship between desired levels of privacy and actual levels of privacy, as illustrated in Figure 3.

In terms of levels of crime it appears that fear of crime bears little relation to actual levels of crime in a community (Halpern, 1995), leading to a psychological explanation in terms of cognitive appraisal. In other words, it is the subjective appraisal of potential crime which is important in the process. Subjective or cognitive appraisal refers to the way in which we evaluate, interpret and give meaning to what we perceive. Thus though we may have little or no evidence of actual crime levels in an area, the appearance of the area, and rumours we have heard, coupled with past experiences in other areas, will lead us to construct a personal view of the area. In this way we may feel frightened in an area which in fact has a very low crime rate. As a naive stranger I once carried out some research which involved visiting areas of London with high levels of unemployment. My experience of the areas and people bore little resemblance to the reactions I got from friends who had spent sufficient time in London to have formed some impression of the different areas.

Perceptions and ultimately fear of crime do not occur in the absence of external factors. It appears that factors such as the presence of strangers in a community, the level of physical in-civilities (such as boarded-up houses, graffiti-covered walls, etc.)

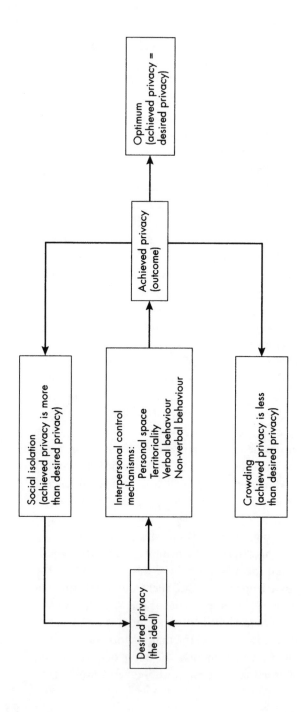

FIGURE 3 Privacy as the central process in the regulation of space

Source: After Altman (1975)

and social incivilities (such as gangs of young people on street corners) have become associated in the public consciousness with crime and translate into cues for fear in the **phenomic** (subjective) **world** of many individuals.

Our sense modalities (hearing, smell, vision, taste and touch) help us to deal with the external world and can adapt to changes over our lifetime. For example, we can develop a taste for particular foods. However, prolonged exposure to stimulation which exceeds our various sense capacities can be stressful. The most widely researched is hearing and noise. Living in a high-noise environment such as near a busy airport (Herridge, 1974) or near a busy motorway (Halpern, 1995) has been shown to increase the risk for psychiatric disorder. There is evidence that we habituate to chronic physical stressors such as noise, which suggests that the stressful consequences may occur in the period before habituation. However, it is not clear whether habituation removes the stressful effects completely. In addition, the combined effect of noise, odour, air pollution, weather and so on is likely to increase the effects of other sources of stress (Cassidy, 1997).

Higher levels of analysis

Traditionally psychologists have focused on the individual level in seeking explanations and analysing human behaviour and experience. However, it is clear that the demands placed upon individuals and the resources which aid coping occur not just at the level of individual factors, but also in group-level factors (family, peer group, work group), societal or organisational-level factors (social attitudes, management attitudes) and cultural-level factors (adapting to a new culture). It is common in the literature to refer to levels of analysis in terms of a hierarchy with the individual level at the bottom and societal or cultural levels at the top. This does not imply any value differential. Thus reference to higher levels does not mean that societal levels are thought to be better than group or individual levels, just different.

What is common to most of the research cited above on external events and stress, whether in terms of life events, cataclysmic events, ambient stressors, etc., is the tendency to focus on the immediate environment. Heller (1989) points out the limitations of a purely individual level of analysis. As he says, we tend to focus on things like difficulty in getting up in the morning, sleeplessness and queasy stomachs, and ignore things like political apathy, how safe people feel on the streets, and the number of people they know by first name. The incorporation of higher levels of analysis leads to the conclusion that problems (in this case stress) are not just problems for individuals but are problems for groups, communities, societies and even cultures. Focusing on the individual level has the potential to engage us in blaming the victim. In other words, we may begin to assume that sources of stress are largely the individual's own fault. For example, traditional individual-level analysis of the causes for eating disorders such as anorexia nervosa often left the anorexic individual feeling even more guilty and hence less likely to recover. Recognising the role of family relations, peer pressure, social models of the ideal body shape and media preoccupation with dieting helps the individual to find a more realistic view of the problem and provides a more comprehensive and valid explanation.

Similarly, in the area of post-traumatic stress disorder (PTSD) in service personnel the condition is often exacerbated by the culture of service organisations (e.g. the fire service), which often views psychological distress as personal weakness. Thus one cannot understand a stress response outside the context within which it is generated, and this requires an understanding of much more than the immediate and obvious context.

Central to the different levels of analysis is the fact that people are social beings operating in a complex social context. In terms of stress that adds the complexity that sometimes what happens to others may be a source of stress for us. Parents, for example, may experience much of their stress through what happens to their children. Life event or daily hassle checklists do not ask about events such as children awaiting examination results or having relationship problems. My daughter recently decided to take up parachute jumping as a hobby at university, something that has at times been a stressor for me.

The issue of children leads on to another neglected aspect of the assessment of stress in the external environment, the developmental aspect. Clearly, researchers acknowledge that children will be exposed to different sources of stress as compared with adults and the elderly. However, even these categories are much too broad. Arguably each decade of adulthood brings different sources of stress. The developmental aspect is important in another sense, in that any situation we encounter has within it a process of ongoing change. The obvious examples are relationships, work and unemployment. Breaking up with someone we have been with for only a couple of weeks will be a different experience from breaking up with a partner of 20 years standing. The literature on unemployment has considered the different psychological effects after different periods of time and found a range of effects from relief to clinical depression and even suicide. Such variation over time can probably never be captured by measures of external stress, but the issues need to be addressed.

Culture, society and social identity

As I write this, the world is mourning the tragic death of Diana, Princess of Wales. It is difficult to describe the extent of grief that is being exhibited across the world. Many people who would have experienced her only as an image through the extensive press coverage she received over the past fifteen or so years and not known her directly as a person are so grieved that they require counselling. Such is the power of global communication systems that they can create relationships and become the source of stress on a global scale. This highlights the need to consider external events at all levels in understanding the stress process. In the popular press recently I read of individuals who have become so saddened by the negative events in the world generally that they are often unable to go out. The term 'compassion fatigue' was being used. There is some evidence that viewing scenes of disaster shown increasingly on television these days has a major effect on our perceptions of the world generally (Bluhm, 1992).

Social representations

There is evidence that health and illness differ across various groups. Males and females differ in the types and levels of illness experienced, as do social and occupational classes. It is a criticism of the stress literature that these differences have only recently begun to be studied, though in defence one might argue that new methodological developments, particularly **structural equation modelling** (SEM), have made the analysis easier. Arguably the life situations of different social groups provide different contexts with substantially different potential sources of stress (Pearlin, 1989). That sources of stress differ significantly across groups within one culture raises the issue of differences across cultures. Cultural differences have not attracted widespread research attention but it is clear they are important when one looks at studies on specific events. For example, studies looking at the stress consequences of crowding suggest that cultures which experience high population densities are less likely to experience stress from crowding (Cassidy, 1997) – just as a person who has previously shared a small office with two people will experience the move to sharing a larger office with one person as a positive move, while the person moving from an individual office will experience sharing as a source of stress. While these cultural differences more obviously relate to appraisal processes (discussed on p. 101), the configuration of potential sources of stress within particular social and cultural contexts needs to be considered in any explanation of stress.

Community psychologists have recognised the importance of considering factors such as fear of crime in a community in explaining and treating mental illness in the community. In fact, as an example fear of crime is useful here. Many psychologists feel that fear of crime is not only more prevalent, but more important for mental health than actual crime (Halpern, 1995).

What makes a stressor stressful?

Despite the methodological problems it seems undeniable that external events can impose demands upon individuals which ultimately lead to negative health consequences. It is also clear that simply cataloguing events is an unproductive exercise. If we consider the range of events that have been identified as stressors we see that they fall into a number of categories.

One way of categorising events is in terms of their severity, scope and duration (Rotton, 1990). Clearly some events (e.g. bereavement) are more severe than others (e.g. missing a bus). Some events affect only one or a few individuals (e.g. losing my keys) while others affect large numbers (e.g. a major flood). In addition, some events are of short duration (e.g. taking a driving test) while others go on for long periods (e.g. noise from the airport next door). However, you don't have to think for very long before you realise that making the distinction between severe and non-severe, etc. is not always easy and events can have elements of both. For example, is a bereavement of short or long duration as a stressor? Think about how you might categorise other stressors. You will probably find that it is a difficult, futile and not very useful exercise.

On the other hand, we might try to identify what makes a stressor stressful. Researchers tend to agree that common to most if not all stressors are elements of controllability, predictability, threat and loss. In fact, it is often the case that the distinction between the presence or absence of stress rests on the perception of threat. Events that are stressful are seen as threats while those that are not stressful are seen as challenges.

The central aspect in the whole process is seen as control. Events that are threatening or involve loss also tend to remove our ability to control. If we can control them they are not threats. Events that are unpredictable are difficult to control. However, events that are too predictable become boring and can be stressful as well. Thus work underload can be as stressful as work overload. The point is that we can increase the likelihood of correctly predicting whether something will cause stress by considering these dimensions, in particular controllability. However, we can never be confident of predicting that an event will be stressful on the basis of an objective analysis of the event. It is the element of personal meaning, or cognitive appraisal, that has the last say in determining the stress impact of any event.

Summary

In this chapter I have reviewed substantial evidence which supports the conclusion that any event has the potential to be a stressor. We have seen the great variety of ways in which the external world can impose demands on us which for many of us will result in a negative health outcome. We need to know a lot of things about an individual's world if we are to identify the stressors in it. Simply listing events that we or others would generally find stressful is totally inadequate. Similarly, looking at one domain of an individual's life provides a distorted picture. People operate within a context which involves home, work, travel, leisure and possibly many other domains. These domains will impinge on the person from a number of different and interdependent levels.

In addition, events do not occur in isolation from each other. The noise of the train passing will still impinge on me as I search for my lost keys and worry about the row I had with my wife this morning. It is the combination of demands across all life domains, at all levels and in combination with each other that stretch my coping resources. Ultimately, however, it is the meaning of the range of complex and interdependent events in my life that determines their stress impact. We will consider the role of meaning in terms of cognitive appraisal in more detail after we have looked at the way in which the environment might provide resources in living.

Further reading

Because we have covered a range of areas which tend to be treated separately in the literature it is difficult to be very specific about further reading. However, for a review of the core issues the following is useful:

Taylor, S. E., Repetti, R. L. and Seeman, T. (1997). Health psychology: what is an unhealthy environment and how does it get under the skin? *Annual Review of Psychology*, 48, 411–47.

Those interested in specific areas might like to follow up one or more of the texts referenced in the relevant section.

Environmental resources

WHILE THE EVIDENCE IN Chapter 3 identifies the external world as a source of demand and hence potentially a source of stress, in all cases there is the implicit assumption that environments also provide resources which help individuals to cope with stress, or buffer the person against the demands. Identifying change as a potential stressor implies that stability may help to reduce stress or even mean that stress is absent. However, since 'absence of stress is death' (Fontana, 1989: 1) and, as we saw in Warr's vitamin model (Warr, 1987), lack of demands can be stressful, it is not quite that simple, something we will consider later in terms of cognitive appraisal. Yet it is clear that environments have positive effects, something that is often ignored in stress research.

Social support

One area that has attracted attention is social support. Throughout history writers have considered the issue of human relationships in great detail, particularly the ecstasy and agony of love. Being isolated and alone has been associated with loneliness, coldness, sadness, ill health and evil, while being with friends and family is associated with happiness, warmth and well-being. Durkheim (1897/1951) associated the lack of social relationships with increased risk of suicide. The modern field of research on the health effects of social support is generally traced to two major papers by Cassel (1976) and Cobb (1976), respectively. Both researchers argued that social support provides a buffering effect against life stress in that individuals who have more social support were more resistant to life stress.

In community psychology, which had been growing in the USA since the early 1960s, social support was recognised as an important aspect of community mental health. Drawing on socio-logical theory on social support which can be traced back to Durkheim (1897) and exemplified in work such as Young and Willmot's (1957) classic study in the East End of London, researchers realised that the breakdown of social relationships at the community level was associated with many social ills and with physical and mental illness. Research began to show how emotional support from health professionals could help alleviate the consequences for those whose social networks were ineffective (Auerbach and Kilmann, 1977).

The developmental influence of social support was obvious in attachment theory from Bowlby's initiation of the concept in the 1950s (Bowlby, 1951, 1969, 1980) to the work of Rutter (1972). The evidence seems clear that the development of a social and emotional bond between the child and a caregiver is essential for the child's social and emotional development and mental health.

Main effects and buffers

It is clear from these several sources that social support provides the person with a buffer against life stress, which begs the question of whether social support has any benefits for the individual regardless of life stress. In other words, does social support have a main effect on mental health? A main effect would suggest that the absence of social support is a stressor, so that people who otherwise lived a stress-free existence, but who did not have social support, would experience stress. A buffering effect suggests that social support has an effect only where stressors exist, so that if a person had little or no stress in their life it wouldn't really matter whether they had social support. Conversely, if they had a lot of stress in their life, having social support would reduce the impact of that stress. Given the prevalence of potential stressors in an individual's life, it is difficult to disentangle main effects from buffering effects. In order to demonstrate a main effect unequivocally, one needs to show that in a population experiencing no stress those with better social support have better mental health. The difficulty lies in finding a stress-free population. Studies tend to produce mixed findings (Orford, 1992). On the one hand, there is evidence that unemployed individuals with low levels of support (Ullah *et al.*, 1985) and individuals in high-stress jobs who have low support from their spouse (Syrotuik and D'Arcy, 1984) have significantly higher levels of psychological distress than those with high levels of support. Those in high-stress jobs who had low social support were more at risk of death in a study of Swedish men (Falk *et al.*, 1992). This clearly demonstrates a buffering effect.

On the other hand, Kasl and Wells (1985) argue that the studies they looked at did not demonstrate any observable buffering effect. Hanson *et al.* (1989) studied social connections and reported social support among Swedish men, and found that both types of support independently predicted mortality rates. This would seem to indicate a main effect of social support. However, since stress levels were not assessed one cannot be sure. Low social integration and low perceived social support were related to heart disease in a 6-year follow-up study (Orth-Gomer *et al.*, 1993). In a US study of 6,848 adults, Reynolds and Kaplan (1990) found that over a 17-year period absence of social connection predicted cancer prevalence in women but not in men.

A link between social connections and mortality rate was shown in another sample of 2,600 males and females (Vogt *et al.*, 1992). However, in a reanalysis of the same data, Hibbard and Pope (1993) found that social support at work reduced mortality rates only for women. In addition, while social support predicted mortality rates, it was the level of stress rather than social support that predicted the development of coronary heart disease (CHD). This suggests a healing effect for social support rather than a preventive one.

Manipulation of social support in an experimental situation was shown to reduce cardiovascular reactivity to stress (Kamarck *et al.*, 1990). Cardiovascular reactivity is known to be a risk factor for CHD. Social support was manipulated by having or not having a friend present in the laboratory.

Cohen and Wills (1985) conclude that the mixed findings regarding the main versus buffering effect of social support are largely due to methodological differences, in particular the failure in some studies to consider social support as serving more than one function, i.e. being multidimensional. They suggest that for emotional support studies do demonstrate a clear buffering effect. For other types of support such as companionship or practical aid, being embedded in a strong social network may have a direct effect on mental health.

Quality versus quantity, function versus structure

Research on social support can be roughly divided into qualitative and quantitative approaches. The qualitative perspective or functional analysis considers the type of support provided and its function for the person, while the quantitative or structural approach attempts to quantify and describe the structure of the social support network within which the person is embedded. To identify the quantity of social support you have you simply list all the different people you interact with and the frequency of interactions. This is the structure of your social support network. To assess the quality of support you need to ask what these other people do for you: that is, the support function which they fulfil. It might be that some help you to deal with emotional problems, others give advice on money matters, and yet others provide a source of useful information. This gives insight into the qualitative or functional aspects of your support.

Clearly, you could have an extensive network but little real support (little functional support), or alternatively have a small network of close and reliable friends who provide a high quality of support in lots of areas. This distinction was brought home to those investigating affective disorder among abused children some years ago. The problem was that abused children who had lots of caring family and carers around them were just as likely to become depressed as those who had little support. The former had a large quantity of support – or, in technical terms, they had a large support network. However, when researchers began to investigate the children's perceptions of their support they found that those who became depressed felt they had no support, regardless of the number of carers around. Similarly, those who didn't become depressed felt they were emotionally close to those around even if it was just one person. This can be explained in terms of the breaking of an emotional bond between the child and adults in its life. Some children were able to isolate this break to the abuser and still trusted and felt supported by others. The at-risk children tended to generalise this break to all adults and therefore trusted no one and felt unsupported.

Functions of social support

As suggested by Cohen and Wills (1985), social support is a multidimensional construct in that it serves a variety of functions. It is very clear that people can provide support for us on a number of different levels. Theorists have identified a number of different dimensions, including emotional support, material (practical) support, informational support, companionship and esteem support.

Social networks

Tolsdorf (1976) attempted to produce a framework for network analysis in the field of social support in comparing the networks of psychiatric and medical patients. Tolsdorf divided the network into three aspects: structure, content and function. The two main aspects of the structure of the network according to Tolsdorf are size and level of interconnection (termed adjacency density). Content of the network can be divided into relationship density, multiplex relationships, kinship members and kinship linkages. The function aspect was concerned with identifying the number of people serving particular functions for the individual and the balance between the functions served by others for the individual and the functions the individual served for others. Tolsdorf saw the main functions as being support, advice and feedback. As suggested above, this is a rather limited view of the functions of social support.

Another approach to network analysis is provided by Kahn and Antonucci (1980), who coined the phrase 'convoys over the life course', thereby recognising the need not only to identify the support network but to recognise its development over time. Thus a person will have different configurations of networks as they develop, and the network will change as some connections are lost and others gained. Kahn and Antonucci also differentiate between different layers of the network viewed as a concentric circle. Thus there will be immediate family, intimate friendships, etc. in the inner layer (closest to the person), then less intimate friends, work colleagues, and so on through more distant family, professionals and neighbours. The suggestion is that inner layers of the network are likely to be more stable over time, with the outer layers varying with changes in occupation, development through education and so on.

The advantage of the Kahn and Antonucci (1980) model is that while it still tends to focus on the individual level and direct contact it allows modification to include higher levels of analysis. For example, one can draw on Bronfenbrenner's (1979) analogy of nested systems. Bronfenbrenner presents the social context of the individual in terms of four main levels or systems nested within each other. At the micro level are systems with which the person has regular direct contact (e.g. home, school). The next (meso) level consists of two or more micro-level systems and their inter-linkages (e.g. home–school). The next level (the exo level) are systems with which the person has no direct contact (e.g. the school governors, a university board of examiners). While there is no direct contact, these systems can provide support, be a resource or a source of stress for the person. The highest level is the macro level and refers to systems on the large scale such as the current political ideology, the labour market and so on. These are systems within which other systems operate and again have an effect on the individual's life. It is clear that people are more or less embedded with a large and complex social context. While the more distant aspects of this context are not directly experienced in the same way that support from a close friend is experienced, they form part of the individual's world. As we shall see, it is the person's perception of support that has a more direct influence on stress and health, and all of the social context will contribute to the person's appraisal or perception of support.

On the whole it seems clear that both a functional and a structural analysis is required in order to explicate the role of social support. However, this is not the whole picture, because, as we shall see below, social support is subject to individual differences.

Social support, social identity and community

Social support as a person variable will be considered on p. 119 when we discuss cognitive appraisal. However, it is useful here to highlight briefly the research on sense of community and social identity which comes from environmental and community psychology. This research draws heavily on sociological studies such as that of Young and Willmott (1957). The failure of some new town developments in both the UK and the USA (and probably elsewhere) in terms of their effects on mental health and crime inspired research which has generally concluded that what was missing was a sense of community or social cohesion (Cassidy, 1997). It seems that a sense of community identity enables people to feel supported and empowered and as a consequence improves mental health.

Individual differences in social support

It is generally the case that the relationship between measures of social networks and measures of perceived support is weak and variable (Sarason et al. (1987). In addition, measures of social networks are poor predictors of health outcomes, whereas measures of perceived support are quite good predictors (Kessler and McLeod, 1984). The discrepancy between objective measures of social networks and the individual's own perception of support availability in their ability to predict health outcomes leads Sarason et al. (1990) to suggest that social support might be considered a personality variable. What seems to be consistently supported by a large volume of research is that it is the person's internal representation and appraisal of their social support that is most important in mediating the stress process.

However, what should not be forgotten is that that internal representation is acquired through an interaction between the person and their context in the first place. Treating social support as a personality variable does threaten to overlook this. Individual differences in perceived social support are clearly learned. A number of possible explanations are offered as to the process of this learning. One is based on attachment bonding in childhood. There is quite strong evidence that attachment bonding between the child and at least one caregiver (not necessarily the mother) is important for the emotional development of the child (Rutter, 1972; Sluckin et al., 1983). The relationship between early childhood bonding and adult behaviour is less clear since research is confounded by what occurs between childhood and adulthood. Perhaps the best interpretation is that what happens in early childhood in terms of bonding plays an initiating role in the development and maintenance of relationships throughout childhood and adulthood (Hazan and Shaver, 1987; Sarason et al., 1987). Sarason et al. (1990) provide a review and a theoretical model for the development of perceived social support (Figure 4).

Power

A function of social support which is often more implicit than explicit is that it empowers individuals. Being part of a social network helps us to feel less alone and hence more in control of events. We can take collective action. Power, in terms of control and autonomy, has been generally treated as a person variable in psychological research, and as such it is possibly the most important concept to have evolved in explanations of human behaviour and experience. It is central to most, if not all, psychological explanations for health and illness, as we shall see later. It has been identified as a focus of therapy, and the concept of empowerment has attracted growing attention in modern psychology,

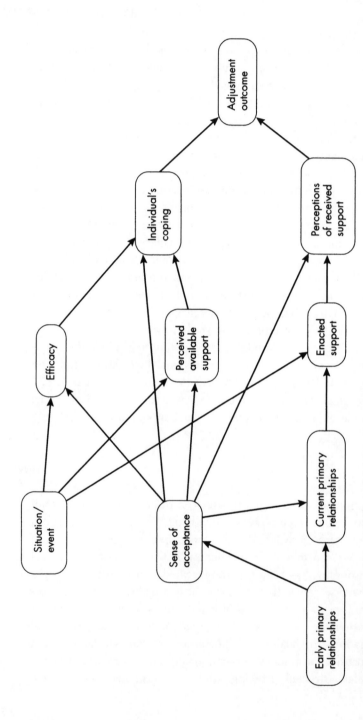

FIGURE 4 A developmental model of social support

Source: Sarasonm Pierce and Sarason (1990)

particularly in critical and feminist perspectives. In sociology, power has been treated as a resource in the social world, a resource which is differentially distributed across groups and individuals. Power organises societies and is arguably the prime motivator, with groups and individuals competing for power in one way or another.

Evolutionary theory is based on competition for resources (whether food or mates) as the main explanatory mechanism for the historical development of all animal species. The role of power in the sense of an external resource has largely been ignored in mainstream psychology. However, a few social psychologists (Ng, 1980; Wrong, 1979) provide a source of information. In addition, the fields of community psychology and environmental psychology have recognised its role. Ultimately I will argue that power and control are determined by the person's cognitive appraisal of their world. However, appraisal does not take place in the absence of external influences, but rather through interaction with the external world. An individual may feel they have no control over events while opportunities for control exist in their world. However, where the external world limits or denies power to the individual, they are less likely to feel in control (though exceptions do exist). Even if they feel in control, the external limitations are likely to change that perception.

Power and decision-making

Power in the external world is inextricably linked to decision-making. In essence it is those who make decisions who exercise power. However, control over decisions is not simple and not always overt. Bachrach and Baratz (1962) identified power which operates to prevent decisions from being made, through manipulation of other's perceptions and keeping issues off the agenda. Ng (1980) adds a third dimension of hidden power as those forces which operate through established social structures by subtly shaping the attitudes and perceptions of people. We can see this sort of power operating where sexist or racist practices are unquestioned. This is the sort of power that Goffman (1961) and others identified in the process of institutionalisation, where individuals are controlled by being made dependent. Power at this level, whether it is exercised through direct impact on decision-making, through passive processes which prevent issues being discussed, or through institutionalised norms which control, is a function of the social and physical environment. It is often part of a role, for example that of a manager at work, or it may be part of the physical environment (e.g. when access to certain buildings or parts of buildings is physically impossible for people with disability, effectively excluding them from a part in decision-making meetings).

The role of power in the work environment has been thoroughly investigated in terms of the processes of leadership (both formal and informal), and generally it is concluded that autonomy and participation in decision-making have positive effects on performance, motivation, commitment, satisfaction and health, and are associated with lower levels of perceived stress. This was demonstrated effectively by Tizard (1975) in a study of nurseries. She compared nurseries where all staff played a full part in decision-making with those where decisions were made by managers with no staff consultation. Not only were the staff in the more autonomous environments happier and less stressed, but so too were their clients, the children. This finding has been replicated in many different types of work organisation.

In relation to the design of physical environments one conclusion stands out above all others: if we are to have physical environments that support positive mental health, the users of the environment must be involved and feel involved in decision-making about the design process at all stages (Halpern, 1995; Cassidy, 1997). Studies have looked at the design of new towns, apartment blocks, neighbourhoods, work buildings, student accommodation and other alterations to physical environments, and the robust conclusion is that where those who were later to occupy the space were involved in the decision-making process from design to completion the environments were more effective. Effectiveness in this context refers to a range of factors, including better mental and physical health, more satisfaction, better work performance, lower levels of crime and a stronger sense of social cohesion. The latter (social cohesion or sense of community) provides a strong explanatory mechanism for differences in levels of mental and physical health, crime and other social problems across different cities, parts of cities or neighbourhoods (Halpern, 1995).

Power and information

Although the issue is not well researched, it is generally widely accepted that control of information is important in the exercise of power. To some extent this is part of decision-making power in that to feel involved in decision-making, people must have access to the necessary information. The role of communication of information has been explored in organisations and it is clear that those who control information hold power, and where communication is free-flowing and effective, workers feel empowered (Greenberg and Baron, 1997). As we shall see, perception of control (a sense of empowerment) is the single most important psychological factor in mediating the stress process. An example of the role of communication in empowering people and reducing stress is in the relationship between health professionals and clients (Ley, 1988). The evidence shows that effective communication with clients, including providing them with information, not only reduces their perceived stress levels and increases their satisfaction, but also influences a range of physical outcomes from the experience of pain to the overall recovery time. It is the way in which the communication process in health service delivery increases client's perceptions of control over the whole experience which is important. In this case it is the social environment (interpersonal communication) which empowers.

Power and the physical environment

An example of the way the physical environment has a direct effect on perceptions of control is in terms of control over access to the self, discussed in the previous chapter. Control over access to the self includes the human need for personal space and privacy and to have control over personal territory. In designing work spaces it was shown that open-plan offices increase absenteeism, reduce worker satisfaction and performance, and are generally deleterious to both physical and mental health (Cassidy, 1997). The best explanation for this effect is that they reduce worker privacy and increase the likelihood of invasion of territory and personal space; that is, they reduce perceived control over access to the self. Providing partitions which allowed workers to reinstate some privacy and to control personal space and territory was effective in alleviating the negative consequences.

This is just one example, but it illustrates effectively how perceived control is influenced by physical environments. In terms of designing residential areas it appears that physical environments which find an appropriate balance between enhancing control over access to the self and enhancing social cohesion have more positive effects on mental and physical health (Halpern, 1995).

Summary

In this chapter we have looked at social support and opportunities for power and control as aspects of the external world which are resources in the stress process. While the evidence is clear that both these factors (support and control) are ultimately determined within the mind of the person in appraising their world, these appraisals do not occur in a total absence of context. Feeling that one is supported and in control is enhanced by particular physical and social environments. In practice the physical and social environment are inseparable, and so too are the processes of support and control. Perceptions of control are enhanced by feeling supported. There has been much less of a focus in psychology on how these external factors operate as resources in the stress process than on the consequences of their absence. We now turn to the person in the process, keeping in mind that the person operates within a physical and social context.

Further reading

For this chapter a useful starting point for further reading might be Chapters 4 and 5 from:

Orford, J. (1992). *Community Psychology*, Chichester: Wiley.

Chapter 5

Personality and stress

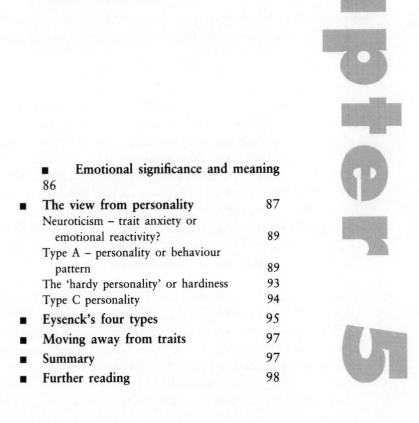

Emotional significance and meaning

While there are some problems associated with the research into external events and health, some general conclusions may legitimately be drawn. It is useful to summarise these here in order to set the context for the role of person factors in the stress process.

First, it appears that any event has the potential to be a stressor. This includes both apparently negative and apparently positive events. Hence holidays, winning a major lottery prize, etc. while on the face of it positive events for most people, are stressful for some and have the potential to be stressful for anyone. In addition, it is not just external events that can be stressors. Internal events such as physiological discomfort, disease or illness and, as we shall see later, internal psychological processes as well, become part of the complex stimuli that impose demands on the person's coping resources. This highlights the interdependent and dynamic nature of the process. While external demands (e.g. a high-stress job) may lead to illness (coronary heart disease), the illness itself (e.g. pain, disruption of family life, etc.) becomes a source of stress. However, just as with external events, its stress impact will be determined by the person's appraisal of their total life situation. For some, illness may represent an escape from an intolerable job and lead to positive life changes. In fact, the developmental process is often ignored. For example, adversity in life if successfully coped with becomes part of the rich tapestry of learning and may later help to reduce the impact of other life stressors.

Second, 'no environmental event can be identified as a stressor independently of its appraisal by the person' (Lazarus and Folkman, 1984: 11). If stress and its consequences could be defined by the objective characteristics of the situation alone, then we should be able to predict the occurrence of stress with great accuracy. However, there is a vast literature which shows clearly that this is not the case. In any given situation which appears to have a number of potential sources of stress, only some of the people in that situation will actually experience stress. Ultimately stressors are defined by their meaning and emotional significance in the phenomic world of the individual.

These two conclusions attest to the importance of individual differences in the stress process. Individual differences in response to stress can be categorised into two research literatures which often overlap. These are research studies which focus on personality and those which focus on cognitive styles. The most important distinction is that personality perspectives tend to assume that the individual difference traits or characteristics are relatively stable over time and across situations, and at their most extreme assume that these traits are genetically inherited. The cognitive style perspective focuses on the patterns of thought that individuals engage in, patterns which can be relatively stable, but which are clearly the product of learning and which are open to change and modification. One of the major problems in the area is that theorists often do not make the distinction.

The view from personality

While personality theories focusing specifically on stress are relatively recent in origin, the relationship between personality and both mental and physical illness have been around for a much longer time. Hippocrates (380 BC) linked personality types with mood and health in terms of the combination of black and yellow bile. In fact, many of the personality theories that have dominated psychological thinking over the past century began as attempts to explain abnormal behaviour or psychiatric disorder. Freud's psychodynamic perspective clearly links personality and health through the individual's attempts to cope with internal conflict, albeit at the unconscious level. The **psychometric approach** to personality is predicated on the assumption that personality types or traits range from normal to abnormal, with some traits such as psychoticism being developed specifically to describe and explain abnormal behaviour. It is assumed that those who score at the extremes on dimensions are prone to psychiatric disorder. In fact, many instruments were derived specifically for clinical diagnoses, for example the Minnesota Multiphasic Personality Inventory (MMPI; Hathaway and McKinley, 1945). Humanistic perspectives too were largely derived from the clinical field. George Kelly (1955), who derived *personal construct theory*, was a clinical psychologist. It is true that many would now feel more comfortable in describing Kelly's theory as a cognitive rather than a personality theory.

Traditional personality theory was challenged effectively through the **person–situation debate**, brought to the fore by Mischel (1968) in his book *Personality and assessment*. Essentially the argument from Mischel and others in what became the interactionist perspective in psychology was that the assumption that traits are stable over time and situation is not supported by the evidence. I do not have the space to cover a general critique of personality in this text, but underpinning our discussion will be a general acceptance of the interactional view. While being critical of the assumptions of temporal and situational stability and the biological reductionism inherent in many traditional personality theories, I would argue that we should not ignore what has been already discovered. Many of the concepts which currently abound are not new but simply reinterpretations of older concepts. The history of psychological theory is strewn with examples of throwing the baby out with the bath water and reinventing the wheel.

Despite the wealth of personality theory around, most writers focus on three main areas of personality in relation to stress, neuroticism and emotional reactivity (Eysenck, 1985), hardiness (Kobasa, 1979), and Type A personality (Friedman and Rosenman, 1974). Only the first of these draws on general personality theory; the other two approaches were developed specifically to explain the stress–health relationship.

Neuroticism – trait anxiety or emotional reactivity?

Neuroticism is a difficult concept in that it is used in the literature as both an independent and a dependent variable. In other
words, it is used as a description of clinical anxiety in the sense
that an individual can be diagnosed as neurotic, and at the same
time it is used as an explanation for disorder. The latter approach
is used in the stress literature, where neuroticism is assumed to
make one vulnerable to life stress. Neuroticism is essentially trait
anxiety, which is assumed to be a relatively stable anxiety proneness. The assumption is that those more prone to anxiety are also
more prone to stress; however, given the use of anxiety as a dependent variable this is something of a tautology. In other words,
people in high-stress situations are by definition more likely to be
anxious, so it really does not add anything to the explanation to
say that anxiety causes stress. In fact, it seems that we might be
better engaged in trying to identify the causal precursors of both
anxiety and the experience of stress, and it will be argued in the
next chapter that both are preceded by the cognitive appraisal
process. In other words, it is the way in which we appraise our
world which produces anxiety and feelings of stress. The concept
of neuroticism was put forward by Eysenck (1957) to explain the
symptoms experienced by war-weary soldiers he encountered in
his work at the Maudsley Hospital in London. These soldiers
were suffering from what would now be called post-traumatic
stress disorder (PTSD). Over the years, neuroticism or trait anxiety
has been linked to a wide range of disorders, and we will revisit
the concept more fully in the next chapter. We will also come
back to Eysenck's view of the link between personality and stress
after first considering two other personality approaches which
were devised specifically to explain stress. These are the concepts
of Type A and hardiness.

Type A – personality or behaviour pattern?

One of the major person factors which has been widely explored
in relation to stress and coping, in particular at work, is the

Type A behaviour pattern (TAB). First introduced by Friedman and Rosenman (1959), TAB has generated an extensive literature and is defined in terms of a cluster of behaviours and characteristics including being extremely competitive, high-achieving, aggressive, hasty, impatient and restless, and in addition exhibiting explosive speech patterns, tenseness of facial muscles and the appearance of being under pressure from time and responsibility (Furnham, 1992). Friedman and Ulmer (1984) describe this as an 'action–emotion complex', which tends to be a useful way of viewing it. In other words, Type A involves an interdependent cluster of emotions and behaviours. Type B is simply defined as the absence of Type A characteristics. TAB has been extensively studied in relation to coronary heart disease (CHD), in which context it was first observed by Friedman and Rosenman (1959).

A confusion has arisen in the literature between Type A behaviour pattern and Type A personality, with the two often being used interchangeably. Some theorists seem to assume that the observed behaviour patterns imply an underlying stable personality trait (Bloom, 1988), while others see them as a function of provoking circumstances (Carroll, 1992). The evidence from intervention studies is that TAB is modifiable (Friedman *et al.*, 1986), which tends to support the **situationist perspective**. In addition, research on TAB at work suggests that the structure of reinforcement in the workplace supports TAB and that as a consequence individuals learn to be Type A (Price, 1982). This suggests that perhaps the best model of TAB is a person-in-context one in which the pattern of behaviours (or 'action–emotion complex') is elicited by the appropriate situational events.

Measurement of TAB tends to be by either questionnaire or structured interview. Three popular questionnaire measures used are the Jenkins Activity Survey (JAS; Jenkins *et al.*, 1979), the Bortner Rating Scale (BRS; Bortner, 1969) and the Framingham Type A Scale (FTAS; Haynes *et al.*, 1978). The Structured Interview (SI) technique currently used was developed by Rosenman (1978) and includes monitoring the style of behaviour exhibited during the interview. Interviews tend to be provocative to increase the likelihood of observing Type A behaviour; in particular, displays of overt hostility are an important factor in interpreting outcomes. Studies suggest that the SI method is the most valid and that the JAS correlates more highly with the SI than do any of the other questionnaire methods. The lack of agreement between measures and the observation that some measures, particularly the FTAS, correlate highly with neuroticism are problems in the area. For a full review of measures see Bennett and Carroll (1989).

Another source of disagreement concerns the effects of TAB. Prospective studies, particularly those using the Structured Interview approach to measuring Type A, tend to produce support for TAB as an independent predictor of CHD (Carroll, 1992). Examples of such studies are the Western Collaborative Group Study (Rosenman et al., 1975), the Framingham study (Haynes et al., 1978) and the French–Belgian Collaborative Group heart disease study (1982). However, some studies (Johnston et al., 1987; Mann and Brennan, 1987; Cohen and Reed, 1985) failed to find a substantial link between TAB and CHD. The Cohen and Reed study looked at Japanese men in Hawaii, which raises the issue of cultural differences, something which has not been researched. In addition, the majority of studies focus on males. This raises the issue of sex differences. There is some evidence that Type A females may cope better than Type A males (Cassidy and Dhillon, 1997).

There is some evidence, too, that Type A individuals may report higher levels of symptoms simply because they are more prone to self-monitoring (Deary et al., 1991). This itself must be interpreted with caution because in the study by Deary and co-workers the higher levels of symptom reporting were among Type As who were also high in neuroticism and low in extroversion, and most significantly among females. It is quite likely that the important factor here was neuroticism rather than Type A. This is to some extent supported by Matthews and Brunson (1979), who found Type As more likely to screen out symptoms as irrelevant and therefore not report them. I have already mentioned the neuroticism–Type A confound in the Framingham Type A Scale.

Two conclusions seem to be supported. First, TAB is a better predictor of the prevalence of CHD than of mortality from CHD. This may be explained in that Type A individuals diagnosed with CHD may change their lifestyles and reduce the risk of mortality, whereas for Type B individuals with CHD such lifestyle changes may not be so accessible.

Second, some aspects of TAB may be more closely associated with risk for CHD than others. One candidate suggested is hostility and anger (Friedman, 1991; Siegel, 1991; Burns and Katkin, 1991).

While a vast literature supports the negative health consequences of TAB, less cognisance has been taken of the positive effects on commitment and performance at work (Phillips *et al.*, 1990). It has been suggested that both Type A and Type B have both positive and negative aspects (Friedman *et al.*, 1985). They identify a non-hostile Type A who is not prone to illness and an over-controlled, inhibited Type B who may be prone to anxiety. This suggests that there may be some important differences within TAB patterns that reflect coping styles.

One area where consensus does appear to exist is in the conclusion that TAB reflects a proneness to stress (Furnham, 1992; Bloom, 1988; Carroll, 1992), whether self-generated or externally imposed, and this increased level of stress is the pathway through which health consequences are mediated. Recent research has begun to focus on other correlates of TAB, for example the finding that Type As have a greater need for control (Furnham, 1990). In fact, Henley and Furnham (1989) suggest that the evidence supports a need to look at the association between TAB and beliefs about the self. This area of beliefs (or cognitive style) is suggested as a fruitful area of investigation in terms of vulnerability or resistance to stress (Lazarus and Folkman, 1984), and has generated a growing literature. In addition, Smith and Rhodewalt (1986) and Smith and Anderson (1986) argue that a transactional alternative to trait approaches to Type A incorporates the idea that Type As create stressful and demanding situations through their choices, cognitions and behaviours. In other words, it is the way in which individuals appraise their situations, i.e. their cognitive style, which determines their tendency to engage in Type A behaviour.

The 'hardy personality' or hardiness

Kobasa (1979) approached the issue from the angle of seeking to identify the relationship between stress and health in terms of the traits that distinguish between stress-resistant and stress-vulnerable individuals. She used the term 'hardiness' to describe a cluster of three dimensions: commitment, control and challenge. Hardiness 'is defined as a personality, cognitive or attributional style that expresses commitment, control and challenge' (Furnham, 1992: 273). I would argue that the concept and its three components are best described in terms of cognitive style. Kobasa clearly sees control, challenge and commitment as learned and open to change, and the concepts are reflected in the work on cognitive styles discussed on pp. 100–27.

Commitment describes the level of involvement in all aspects of life based on the level of belief held in the self and one's purpose.

Control is essentially one's belief about the locus of control over events in life, ranging from internal to external. The concept of control is perhaps the most important psychological variable in the stress process and has generated a vast literature both within and without the stress literature. It is discussed in more detail in the next chapter, but it might be useful to whet the reader's appetite here. When we discussed power and control as external resources in the previous chapter I argued that while the extent to which the external world allows, enhances and enables one to control one's life is a major determinant of stress and its health effects, the appraisal or perception of control supersedes its objective aspects. One can feel in control amid a lack of objective evidence of control, and by doing so negate the health consequences of stress. For example, the car drivers in the commuting research feel more in control than train passengers despite the traffic congestion which they endure. Locating the cause for events in our life within ourselves allows us to feel in control whereas locating causes for events in the hands of others, luck or circumstance means that we do not feel in control. This is what is meant by locus of control, and the personality perspective suggests that people's tendency to locate control internally or externally is a stable personality trait. This view is challenged by the bulk of research discussed in the next chapter.

Challenge reflects a belief in the normality of change, which leads to a tendency to view life's problems as challenges rather than threats.

The fact that all three concepts are based on beliefs (cognitions) about the world supports the argument that they should be considered in terms of cognitive style. The essence of the relationship between hardiness and stress is that the beliefs one holds leads one to cope in particular ways. Thus the person who has strong beliefs in internal control, commitment and challenge will tend to appraise problems as controllable and opportunities to develop.

Type C personality

It has also been proposed that there is a specific personality type associated with cancer, a speculation which apparently dates back to Galen (AD 2), who observed that more melancholic women were more likely to develop breast cancer (Contrada *et al.*, 1990). Although heavily criticised on methodological grounds (Fox, 1978), studies using a range of methods including case-control, retrospective and prospective approaches have produced some evidence of characteristics associated more frequently with cancer. This cluster has been termed the cancer-prone personality or Type C. Contrada *et al.* (1990: 656) state that Type C 'is thought to represent a coping style that is the converse of that displayed by Type A individuals, with Type B falling in between the other two on a continuum'. Type B was previously defined as the absence of Type A behaviour. With the addition of Type C it now seems to be defined as the absence of both Type A and Type C behaviour. Type C seems to be identified particularly by a proneness to depression, high levels of helplessness/hopelessness, poor social support and low emotionality (Contrada *et al.*, 1990).

The area of emotions and Type C is of particular interest in that it has been explored from a number of angles and it forms the basis for the Eysenck types discussed in the next section. It appears that cancer-prone individuals are more likely to distance themselves or disengage emotionally from their experiences (Wirsching et al., 1982). They report lower levels of neuroticism and anxiety (Kissen et al., 1969), appear more fatalistic (pessimistic) (Greer et al., 1979), and more likely to repress their feelings (avoidance or denial) (Jensen, 1987). In contrast to Type A, the Type C individual exhibits less hostility and is less likely to express anger openly (Jansen and Muenz, 1984). The evidence for the link between emotional expression and cancer is based largely on comparisons between those who survive for a relatively long period after diagnosis and those who succumb sooner to the disease. Furthermore, the link between factors like emotional expression, helplessness/hopelessness and cancer is thought to be through the immune system function, and particularly the NK cell function discussed on p. 25. It thus appears to be very similar to the stress and coping influence on biological processes postulated in the area of psychoneuroimmunology.

An important confounding factor in the Type A and Type C literature is that Type A studies have been predominantly of male participants, while Type C studies have tended to focus on females. It could be argued that Type A behaviour is supported by socialisation in males, while Type C behaviour reflects the socialising pressures on females (Contrada et al., 1990).

Eysenck's four types

Eysenck (1985) argues that personality and stress both affect health in direct and indirect ways. On the basis of his three-factor theory of personality, particularly the dimensions of neuroticism and extraversion and their several combinations, and on his research on low emotional expressiveness and cancer (Kissen and Eysenck, 1962), he and his colleagues proposed a number of personality types that relate to health and illness

(Grossarth-Maticek *et al.*, 1988). In essence this classification was aimed at clarifying the relationship between personality, heart disease and cancer in particular. The four types identified by Grossarth-Maticek *et al.*, (1988) are as follows:

- Type 1: *Underestimation.* People of this type appear to become emotionally dependent on things or people in their lives but to be unable to deal with their emotional attachment successfully. As a result they have a sense of uncontrollability, helplessness and hopelessness. Such people are of the emotionally inexpressive cancer-prone personality type.

- *Type 2: Over-arousal.* People of this type are also emotionally dependent on objects and people in their lives, but react to their inability to attain the objects or people with hostility, anger and aggression. These are the hostile, coronary heart disease-prone (Type A) people.

- *Type 3: Ambiguous.* People of this type waver between types 1 and 2 and back again, thus alternating between lack of control, hopelessness and helplessness, and anger, hostility and aggression. They are considered essentially healthy.

- *Type 4: Personal autonomy.* This people type tend to be in control of their own destiny, not dependent on objects or people, and essentially cope well with life stress.

Although this model is based on empirical evidence, it is hard to see what it adds to explanations of the stress process. Perhaps the important core of this research is the evidence for a relationship between one's emotionality and stress. It appears that the key to being healthy is to be in control of one's emotions. The emotionality element draws heavily on Eysenck's model of neuroticism and can be best viewed as an outcome of the cognitive appraisal process discussed in the next chapter. The authors bring into their description of the four types the concepts of control, hopelessness, helplessness and approach–avoidance tendencies. These are all concepts that have been explored from a cognitive perspective and are discussed in the next chapter.

Moving away from traits

Contrada *et al.* (1990) argue that personality theory in the health fields must move away from a trait approach and adopt a more flexible process approach if it is to be useful. Their arguments include the need for an interactional or transactional analysis between person and situational factors, the importance of cognitive and motivational processes, and the relationship between dispositions and coping. In fact, it seems as if this process approach dispenses with the need for explanations in personality terms at all, and fits more comfortably with the cognitive appraisal, cognitive style perspective discussed in the next chapter. In fact, they draw on the work of people like Lazarus (1966), Abramson *et al.* (1978), Bandura (1977) and Carver and Scheier (1981), whose theories are not really within the personality field. I would argue that concepts such as cognitive appraisal, attributional style, self-efficacy, perceived control and optimism can be much better explained in terms of cognitive style. This is explored in detail in the next chapter.

Summary

In this chapter we have considered the person in the stress process from a personality perspective. To begin with, the assumption that personality traits are stable across time and situation has been widely challenged in psychology in general and in the field of stress and mental health in particular. When traits that have been associated with stress and health are explored more fully it is clear that they can be reformulated effectively in cognitive terms. In fact, there is often little more to be done in reformulating the concepts used but to remove the term 'personality'. While there is no doubt that patterns of behaviour can and do remain relatively stable for periods of time and across some situations, it is equally not doubted that these patterns are subject to change both as part of the developmental process and as a consequence of direct intervention. The limitations of the personality trait approach become more obvious when we explore the cognitive style literature in the next chapter.

Further reading

Again, because of the diverse nature of the literature we have covered it is difficult to be very specific about further reading. There are numerous useful references provided within each perspective covered in the chapter. However, for an overview of the critique of traditional personality perspectives which forms the backbone of the chapter, you might wish to read:

Mischel, W. (1990). Personality dispositions revisited and revised: a view after three decades. In L. A. Pervin (ed.) *Handbook of personality: theory and research*, New York: Guilford Press.

Cognition and stress

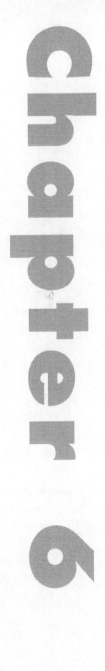

THE COGNITIVE REVOLUTION OR return of mind to psychology is generally identified as having got under way in the 1970s (Lazarus, 1993). However, to suggest that no cognitive theories of behaviour and experience existed prior to that would be a gross inaccuracy. The role of cognitive processes in terms of beliefs was not a problem for the more eclectic theorists in psychology right from its inception. People like James (1890), Murray (1938), Lewin (1935) and others assumed that cognitive processes were an important part of any explanation of human behaviour and experience.

In the longer term, philosophy, from which psychology as a discipline developed, has been preoccupied with the role of cognition in terms of reason and thought. By connecting belief and motivation in his definition of anger Aristotle may well be the first to have provided a cognitive theory of emotion (Lazarus, 1993). For Descartes it was the ultimate existential evidence: 'I think, therefore I am.' In literature, many of the discoveries of modern cognitive psychology were much better expressed down the ages. For example, when Shakespeare through Hamlet suggests, 'there is nothing either good or bad, but thinking makes it so' (Hamlet, Act II, Scene 2, line 259), he is encapsulating the essence of cognitive psychology.

Lazarus, whose work could be said to provide the synthesis of this perspective in stress research, acknowledges the historical development of what he calls the cognitive-mediational perspective in the following quote;

> The outlook was anticipated by many illustrious figures in North American psychology, including Asch, Harlow, Heider, Kelly, McClelland, Murphy, Rotter and White, as well as their intellectual mentors, Lewin and Murray, and still others who worked within the psychoanalytic

framework. We often forget too that this outlook dominated classical Greek and European thought.

(Lazarus, 1993: 7)

However, it was the failure of attempts to explain human behaviour without incorporating cognitions, and the attempts experimentally to define aspects of the cognitive process, which made the 1970s so important for cognitive theory. In the stress field workers such as Lazarus (1966) had clearly identified the central role of cognitive appraisal processes. In addition, the interactionist critique of traditional personality theory spawned by Mischel's (1968) book led theorists to look towards cognitive processes for explanations for individual differences. It is within this cognitive (or cognitive–behavioural) field that we find the roots of many of the most important explanatory variables used in stress research currently.

The appraisal process

It was the seminal work of Lazarus and his colleagues (Lazarus, 1966; Lazarus and Folkman, 1984) which brought the role of cognitive appraisal to prominence in stress research. The combined effect of the two major conclusions from a wealth of research which supported the role of cognitive appraisal were that any environmental event has the potential to be a stressor, and that no event can be identified as a stressor outside of the person's appraisal of the event. Cognitive appraisal as a concept places the person at the centre of their world and at once combines the Gestalt tradition in psychology with its emphasis on meaning (Kohler, 1940; Koffka, 1935) with the **constructivist perspective** in mainstream cognitive psychology (Neisser, 1976; Gregory, 1973) and the original constructivism of George Kelly (1955). It is founded on the phenomenological and existential strands in philosophy, and deals with Allport's (1955) inside–outside problem by placing the dominant focus on the world inside the mind, the phenomic world. Whether through personal constructs, blueprints, mental maps or cognitive schemata, the phenomic world attends to, filters, processes, stores and gives meaning to information, and ultimately guides responses to the external world.

The cognitive-mediational approach

The next goal in stress research is therefore to define the appraisal process and identify how it influences the process of stress. Lazarus sees appraisal as the process that mediates or actively negotiates between environmental demands and resources and the goal hierarchy and personal beliefs of the person (Lazarus, 1993). Initially appraisal was divided into two aspects: primary appraisal, which involves an evaluation of whether a problem exists; and secondary appraisal, which involves an evaluation of one's resources in dealing with the problem. In other words, in a stressful encounter I need first of all to recognise that a potential stressor is present, and second, I need to identify any resources I have to deal with the stressor. The outcome of the appraisal process will be a coping response (including possibly a non-response). Halpern (1995) argues that a third type of appraisal needs to be distinguished; that is, the appraisal of control, which involves an evaluation of the cause for the problem. This can be in terms of the internal–external continuum discussed on p. 109, or the failure to locate any cause, resulting in a sense of helplessness.

Lazarus defines appraisal as a negotiation between demands and the goal hierarchy and personal beliefs of the person, thus identifying the role of motivation and existing cognitions in the process. To take the motivational element, the evaluation of threat will be directly related to the person's commitment to whatever is being threatened. Hence someone who has a strong commitment to profit in business is likely to appraise any threat to that profit as a stressor. The goals people aspire to, the value of those goals and the effort they are willing to expend to attain those goals give a measure of commitment.

In terms of personal beliefs or existing cognitions we are concerned essentially with the attribution of meaning and the phenomic world which the person has constructed to that point in time. Lazarus identified beliefs about control as central in a belief system.

Lazarus and colleagues (Lazarus, 1966, 1968; Lazarus *et al.*, 1970) applied an experimental paradigm to the investigation of cognitive-mediational aspects of stress. They created the stress situation by presenting stressful films in laboratory settings and monitored stress responses by both subjective report and physiological recordings of heart rate and electrical activity in the skin. Those watching the films recorded significant increases in both subjective and physiological measures of stress. A typical film depicted bloody accidents such as a finger being cut off by a circular saw under the guise of accident prevention. Prior to watching films, participants were prepared by listening to one of several alternative recorded passages. These ranged from denial ('people in this film were not actually injured'), through distancing ('the accidents portrayed are used to teach people how to avoid accidents'), to stress inducing ('people in this film suffered severe pain and infection'). In later studies, stress was induced by leading people to believe they were going to see some horrendous event but never actually showing it. In both the denial situation and the distancing condition the films produced significantly smaller increases in stress responses than the stress-inducing condition. This was interpreted as showing that providing people with ways to appraise the situation in less threatening ways allowed them to reduce the stress impact. From these studies Lazarus and his colleagues showed that the level of stress experienced was mediated by the cognitive styles of participants.

The approach of Lazarus and colleagues was heavily influenced by the expectancy-value perspective, which was popular in social cognition in the early 1970s, and this influence is clear in their identification of motivation and beliefs as the central aspects of cognitive-mediational processes. **Expectancy-value models** assume that the likelihood of a behaviour occurring is a function of the value to the person of the goal at which the behaviour is aimed, and the expectation that the behaviour will be successful in attaining the goal. So if I value the goal of losing weight and I believe (or expect) that dieting will be effective in helping me to lose weight, then I am more likely to diet than if I do not value the goal and/or do not believe that dieting will accomplish it. Thus the behaviour of dieting is largely determined by my motivation and beliefs.

Beliefs and cognitive styles

We have seen that when personality theorists attempt to explain stress and individual differences in health they are forced to draw on the concept of belief, and indeed most, for example Kobasa, tend to describe their concepts in terms of cognitive styles. Theorists talk about beliefs about control, beliefs about goals and values in terms of commitment or strength of need and so on. For many others, in the tradition of Lazarus, individual differences in the stress process are clearly best explained in cognitive terms. Individual differences in the stress field can be broadly defined as personal vulnerability or resistance to external sources of stress. In the literature a number of different, often presented as competing, theoretical perspectives on vulnerability have evolved. Examples include locus of control, attributional style and problem-solving style, all of which are discussed later in the chapter. Much of the theory did not develop within the stress field, but rather as attempts to explain various clinical phenomena, particularly depression, as in the attributional style (Abramson et al., 1978) and problem-solving style (Nezu, 1987; Nezu et al., 1989) theories of depression. However, it is clear that the processes explicated are very much within the remit of stress since the explanations for depression offered are based on the way in which the attributional style, locus of control, problem-solving style and so on mediate the effects of external demands or stressors.

The tendency for theorists to explicate and then defend their particular theory has hampered any attempt to integrate the different models. Arguably these perspectives can be categorised under a limited number of themes, and as integrative research continues to develop they may come to be subsumed by an even smaller number of categories. At the present time the dominant themes identifiable are *perceived control, perceived social support, attributional style, problem-solving style, achievement motivation* and *commitment, emotional reactivity,* and *optimism/pessimism.* It is argued here that all other research approaches can be encompassed within these seven categories. We shall discuss the main tenets of each of these perspectives in the stress context and then consider how the different perspectives might be related.

Control

'In research on stress, loss of control is one of the few forms of psychological trauma that researchers can agree is universally aversive' (Skinner, 1995: 3). We have seen how controllability was perhaps the main aspect of any event which differentiates between a stressor and a non-stressor, and how power as an external resource impinges on the stress process. We now turn to control as an aspect of the person, perceived power. The role of control in the psychology of the person has been identified in personality theories from McDougall's *self-assertion,* through Maslow's *dominance feeling* to McClelland's *power motive.* In this tradition it appears as a need that differentiates individuals in that some have more need to have power, to be in control or to dominate than others. In Kobasa's hardiness theory control is identified as one of the three important factors, and in the Type A theory an important aspect of Type A behaviour is a high need for control.

As Skinner (1995) points out, over fifty years of research has supported the concept in almost every aspect of human behaviour and experience including motivation, emotion, performance, interpersonal behaviour, problem-solving, health, psychiatric disorder and stress. In fact, it is difficult to find an area of human behaviour and experience where control has not been identified as an important causal factor in one way or another. However, it was with the recognition that perceived control is about beliefs or cognitions that the concept has really evolved and found a place as a dominant theme in understanding the stress process. A number of historical themes have come together in the development of the concept. The first of these is learned helplessness.

Learned helplessness

The concept of learned helplessness emerged from the work within the behavioural paradigm carried out by Martin Seligman and his colleagues (Seligman, 1975; Seligman and Maier, 1967). In studies where dogs were given inescapable electric shocks it was shown that they stopped trying to escape, even when put in situations where escape was again possible. They had learned to feel helpless. The fact that this behaviour appeared similar to the withdrawal and apathy observed in depressed humans, and that the learned helplessness in the dogs responded to treatment by drugs used to treat depression in humans, led to the proposition that this could be used to explain human depression. The explanation was that depression in humans occurs as a result of learning that the consequences of one's behaviour are not under one's own control. Just like the dogs in the inescapable shock condition, life deals us a raw deal and we cannot change it, so we withdraw and become depressed. We feel that we have no control over the consequences of our behaviour, so why should we even try?

Attributional style

Abramson *et al.* (1978), in response to critiques of the behavioural emphasis of the learned helplessness theory, presented a reformulation in terms of attributional style. Critics of the learned helplessness model felt that there must be more than just the direct impact of external events, since while learned helplessness does occur for many who are in stressful life situations, it does not occur for everyone. Clearly there must be some internal process that protects some people. In trying to identify this internal process Abramson *et al.* came up with attributional style. They suggested that the cognitive process which intervened between observed non-contingency of behaviour and consequence and the learned helplessness involved attributions about causes for the non-contingency. In other words, people differ in whether they do actually feel helpless.

Abramson *et al.* (1978) suggested that attributions were made on three dimensions: internal–external, stable–unstable and global–specific. Individuals who made external, stable and global attributions for non-contingency were more vulnerable to life stress and prone to depression. The attribution of external causality involves believing that events are outside our control, in the hands of others or down to luck or fate. This fatalistic view suggests that we cannot do anything about this stressful life situation. The stable–unstable dimension reflects attributions about temporal stability, in that the cause ranged from 'always likely to be present' to 'just limited to this particular instance'. In essence, if I feel that things are beyond my control I may also feel that they will always be beyond my control. The global–specific dimension relates to situational stability and follows the reasoning that no matter where I go things will be outside my control. It is easy to see that if I make global attributions (things will always be outside my control) and stable attributions (no matter where I go things will be outside my control), I am being pessimistic. Alternatively, I could feel that I will one day take control and/or if I move to a new situation I will be in control, and I would then be described as optimistic. The internal–external dimension reflects attributions about control. Attributions about temporal and situational stability reflect a dimension of optimistic versus pessimistic thinking. If I am in a stressful job and I feel no control and become pessimistic, I am prone to depression.

Alloy *et al.* (1988), in line with the arguments above, again modified the learned helplessness–attributional style perspective of Seligman and colleagues under the rubric of the hopelessness theory of depression. They suggested that the outcome of the attributional process was a sense of hopelessness rather than helplessness. In other words, the important aspect of perceived lack of control is whether it is linked with a pessimistic or an optimistic outlook.

I have listed attributional style as a separate theme in the current literature, but as follows from the above discussion it would appear that it seems mainly to hinge on two other themes, control and optimism, each with a literature of its own, and it is likely that attributional style will be subsumed by these alternative concepts. The vast literature that has grown around the attributional style perspective provides a great deal of support for its role as a mediator of the stress process (Brewin, 1985; Sweeney *et al*, 1986). The evidence is that those who tend to respond to external stressors by making external, global and stable attributions are more likely to develop psychological and physical illnesses.

Attributions by a different route

While Seligman and colleagues arrived at their attributional style theory through a search for the explanation for learned helplessness, Weiner and colleagues (Weiner, 1986, 1990; Weiner *et al.*, 1978, 1979) drew on the substantive literature on attributions in the field of social cognition. Originating with Heider (1958), the concept of attribution had found a central role in the social psychology of the 1970s. The development of theory on how the lay person attributes causes for their own and other's behaviours had identified a number of important dimensions in the process, the most consistent being the internal–external dimension. Weiner identified four dimensions that were important in regard to emotions. In addition to the internal–external dimension he suggested stability, controllability and intentionality. He distinguished between internal–external attributions and attributions of controllability in that one might attribute a cause as being internal but still not see it as controllable. The stability dimension he saw as being important in terms of expectancy about future behaviour, again similar to the notion of optimistic versus pessimistic thinking. Intentionality was an additional and important dimension concerned with identifying responsibility in others. The stress-prone individual would be the person who made external attributions, or in cases of internal attributions felt they were uncontrollable, had a pessimistic expectation for the future and tended to see the thwarting actions of others as intentional and deliberate.

Locus of control

Working within a social learning paradigm, J. B. Rotter (1966) proposed the concept of locus of control to distinguish between perceptions of behaviour that is under our own control and behaviours which are due to luck or under the control of others. The concept was proposed as part of an expectancy-value model of behaviour. Expectancy-value models are utilised to predict the likelihood of particular behaviours occurring. In essence, if the individual expects to attain a goal by performing a behaviour, and if the goal is valued, they are more likely actually to engage in the behaviour. Locus of control became divorced from the rest of the model and attracted a great deal of attention as an individual difference variable, enhanced by the measuring instrument which Rotter developed. It is arguably unfortunate that the internality–externality dimension of locus of control began to be treated as a personality trait. Rotter was working within a behavioural perspective and saw the internal–external dimension as a function of whether behaviour was under the control of internal or external cues.

The classic example is some very successful applications of Rotter's locus of control approach to eating behaviour. Explanations for obesity were couched in terms of responding to external rather than internal cues. The obese person tends to respond to cues like the time on the clock to instigate eating. In this way, if it is one o'clock it is lunchtime and I eat whether or not I am hungry. This is in contrast to the person who responds only to internal cues such as hunger pangs and therefore eats only when they are hungry. Again the obese person's cue to stop eating is external, e.g. the plate is empty, while the alternative is to respond to internal cues, such as feeling full. Training people to respond to internal rather than external cues has had some success in dealing with obesity, and other appetitive problems such as alcoholism. Clearly the model suggests that people can change from external to internal, which does not fit with the notion of internality–externality as a stable personality trait.

We can see that all the above approaches were essentially predicated on the concept of perceived control. Between them they provide overwhelming evidence from both animal and human studies that perceiving oneself as being in control is important in mediating the effects of a stressful life situation. For a good review see Skinner (1995).

Skinner (1995) argues very elegantly that the roots of perceived control lie in an innate competence need. The argument is that humans (and other animals) are born with a need to master their world in order to survive. Thus competent interactions are rewarding and lead to a sense of personal control. As cognitive development occurs, cognitive processes fit within this basic need for control and organise our perceptions of the external world in a way that enhances our feelings of control. In fact, the highest level of cognitive processing, referred to in cognitive psychology as the metacognitive processes, operates to impose control on lower-level cognitive processes. Thus we can decide what to think about and what to ignore and even to stop a train of thought once we recognise that it exists. Such *thought-stopping ability* is utilised very effectively in cognitive treatments for depression (see the next section). Whether we believe that the impetus for control lies in an innate need for competence, a survival instinct, the drive to seek pleasure and avoid pain, or the drive for self-actualization, it seems that a good case can be made for some sort of initial biological drive. However, the sense of control (or lack of control) develops through the individual's experience of their interaction with the external world. These interactions are reworked into internal representations which incorporate as a central aspect different levels of perceived control.

Optimism/pessimism

While it seems clear that perceived control has been well established as an important aspect of the cognitive mediation of stress,
it is strongly argued that a second core theme comes out of the
attributional style perspective in the form of a sense of hope or
optimism versus a sense of hopelessness or pessimism. Weiner
(1990) argues that the stability dimension (optimism–pessimism)
in attribution theory is more important than the internal–external
(control) dimension. Alloy *et al.* (1988) identify hopelessness as
the outcome of the attribution process for the depression-prone
individual. The evidence supporting both Weiner and Alloy *et al.*
is that those who make optimistic attributions (i.e. are more
hopeful) fare better with life stress than those who make
pessimistic attributions.

Beck (1976), in his cognitive theory of depression, identifies
hopelessness as the central theme for the depression-prone person.
Beck's theory of depression is in terms of a *cognitive triad*, in
which the depressed person has a negative view of themselves,
their world and their future. Again from a different source, i.e.
working with clinical patients, we find a similar theme emerging.
The argument is that this negative thinking is in response to
external demands or life stress, and the person who thinks in this
way cannot cope with life stress. For Beck the essence of the
negative cognitive triad was a pessimistic attitude or a sense of
hopelessness. In fact, Beck's theory is essentially based on
pessimistic versus optimistic thinking about the self, the world
and the future. Beck (1976) developed a cognitive–behavioural
approach to therapy which in many ways revolutionised the treatment of depression. It involves training patients to recognise a
negative train of thought, to be able to stop the train (thought
stopping), and to replace it with a more positive thought. Patients
are rewarded, and learn to self-reward for effectively engaging in
this process.

In regard to the relationship between optimism and depression there is a strong argument that the optimism displayed by
those who enjoy positive well-being is in fact unrealistic. In other

words, those who become depressed are not so much pessimistic as realistic, having lost the ability among non-depressed individuals to place a positive bias on things. This debate is also taken up in the health arena in the suggestion that the reason many people engage in unhealthy lifestyles is that they have an inaccurate perception of risk (Weinstein, 1984). This is expressed in terms of the *fundamental attribution error*. This refers to our tendency to attribute the cause for our own bad behaviour to circumstance (I was unlucky to fail the exam) and other's bad behaviour to themselves (you failed the exam because you lack intelligence). In addition, we attribute our own good behaviour to ourselves (I passed the exam because I am intelligent) and other's good behaviour to circumstance (you passed the exam because you were lucky). As a concomitant of this we tend to assume that terrible things happen only to other people, not to us. This is partly explained by the *just world hypothesis*, the belief that bad things happen to bad people. We are not bad therefore we won't catch that nasty disease. It is perhaps best explained in terms of unrealistic optimism, i.e. the ability to see our own life and future through rose-tinted spectacles. Since optimism–pessimism is generally measured as a single bipolar dimension it is difficult to reach any conclusion as to whether the literature suggests that ineffective coping is the result of the presence of pessimism or the absence of optimism.

In a separate literature inspired mainly by the work of Scheier and Carver (1987, 1992), optimism has been investigated as a core disposition. They see optimists as more likely to feel that desired outcomes are within their reach, a sort of future-oriented sense of control. Using the Life Orientation Test (LOT), a measure of dispositional optimism, Scheier and Carver (1985) and Scheier *et al.* (1986) have produced evidence that optimists are more stress resistant and that this resistance is the result of better coping strategies. Aspinwall and Taylor (1992), in a longitudinal study of college students, found that optimists were less likely to use avoidance coping. Optimism as measured by the LOT seems to be related to neuroticism (Smith *et al.*, 1989), which may confound the optimism–stress relationship somewhat. In other words, it may be that some of the variance in stress attributed to optimism may in fact be accounted for by neuroticism. This is similar to negative affectivity critique of life events measures offered by Watson and Pennebaker (1989).

The treatment of optimism as a disposition also attracts the same criticisms as the trait approach to locus of control. Once we begin to describe optimism as a trait we get into the problem of assuming temporal and situational stability and we as theorists are left with a rather pessimistic or fatalistic view of the process. The more optimistic view is that optimism is a cognitive style which, while demonstrating some consistency, is sensitive to situational and temporal influence. Thus the person who is optimistic in one situation may become pessimistic in another situation or at another time. The fact that pessimistic thinking can be changed by therapeutic intervention as in Beck's cognitive–behavioural therapy tends to support the more flexible cognitive style view. In other words, optimism–pessimism is best defined as a style of thinking (cognitive style) which is learned and open to change.

From the discussion of cognitive style so far it can be concluded that control and optimism–pessimism (hopelessness) are well established in both research evidence and the practice of clinical psychology. Arguably these two concepts can subsume the attributional style perspective. However, there may be some utility in not discarding the attributional style yet, at least until more integrative research can show that it has become obsolete. The theme of hope–hopelessness, or optimism–pessimism, will be revisited when we consider motivation later in the chapter. First of all let us consider another approach to defining cognitive styles that mediate the stress process, i.e. the problem-solving style perspective.

Problem-solving style

The problem-solving style perspective is even more recent than the attributional approach. This approach developed from the initial distinction between coping behaviours and the patterns of thinking and appraisal regarding coping that people develop (Billings and Moos, 1981). In many ways this is part of the secondary appraisal process suggested by Lazarus and colleagues, and involves appraisal of the person's coping resources. Nezu *et al.* (1989: 121) define problem-solving style as 'the cognitive–behavioural process by which individuals identify or discover effective strategies for coping with problematic situations encountered in daily living'. Nezu (1987) suggests a five stage process which if engaged in effectively would render the individual resistant to external stressors and less vulnerable to depression. These stages are:

1   problem orientation – the recognition that a problem exists;
2   problem definition and formulation – assessing the extent of the problem and setting realistic goals;
3   generation of alternative solutions;
4   decision-making – choosing the solution to be implemented; and
5   solution implementation and verification – carrying through the chosen solution, monitoring and evaluating its success, and self-reinforcing for success.

The five stages can be seen clearly to span the primary and secondary appraisal processes and provides a link between the two.

The problem-solving style model was developed with a focus on depression, as with attributional style theory. However, it is very clear that it too applies more broadly to the stress process. In a literature search eighty-six different studies were identified covering the period 1985–91 on the topic of problem-solving, stress and affective disorders. The earlier work tended to focus on problem-solving skills using a predominantly behavioural framework. However, although the more recent work has moved to an emphasis on identifying the cognitive processes which underlie the skills, i.e. problem-solving styles, there still tends to be some confusion in the literature between the concepts of problem-solving skill and problem-solving style. Problem-solving skill focuses on the practical skills used in dealing with problems and typically involves giving someone a problem to solve and monitoring the way in which they tackle it. Problem-solving style, on the other hand, refers to the underlying way of thinking that someone develops regarding problems. As such, it is typically assessed by self-report or interview or inferred from observation of behaviour in the real world. The assumption is that positive problem-solving styles will lead to effective problem-solving skills.

A large number of studies support the utility of problem-solving interventions in a range of areas. For example, Denham and Almeida (1987), in a meta-analysis of the theory and practice of problem-solving skills interventions with children, report a robust relationship between interventions and behavioural adjustment. In essence, problem-solving interventions have produced reliable and consistent improvements in the behaviour of children with behaviour problems. Tisdale and Lawrence (1986), in a review of the literature, conclude that the approach has been successful with maladjusted children, emotionally disturbed adolescents and adult psychiatric patients, and suggest that problem-solving skills are predictive of successful life adjustment generally.

The evidence supplied by Nezu et al. (1989), in their comprehensive review, suggests that problem-solving style is not a unitary concept. Other work, by Heppner and Petersen (1982) and Heppner et al. (1987), also identifies the multidimensional nature of the construct. Heppner and Petersen (1982) developed a Personal Problem-solving Inventory which measures three factors: problem-solving confidence, approach-avoidance style and personal control.

Nezu (1987) also identifies the work of Billings and Moos (1981, 1982, 1984, 1985) as an important contribution. These authors tend to talk of coping responses, but one can see from their Coping Responses scale (Billings and Moos, 1981) that they are in fact measuring problem-solving styles.

Cassidy and Long (1996) developed a six-factor measure of problem-solving style and used the scale to show that problem-solving style differentiates between clinical and non-clinical samples and acts as a mediator in the stress process. The six factors identified are (1) a sense of *helplessness* in problem situations, (2) *perceived control* over problems, (3) *creativity* in generating solutions to problems, (4) *confidence* in one's ability to deal with problems, (5) a tendency to *approach* problems, and (6) a tendency to *avoid* problems. Approach and avoidance came out as separate factors, suggesting that the absence of approach is not avoidance. In other words, I may not approach (tackle problems head on), but this does not necessarily mean that I actively avoid them. The data so far suggest that the approach –avoidance relationship is not straightforward. For example, people who score high on approach style are not always the best at coping with stress, an effect which perhaps can be summarised in terms of the adage 'fools rush in where angels fear to tread'. A moderate amount of approach style seems best. On the other hand, conflicting evidence with the avoidance dimension suggests that sometimes avoiding the issue may be a positive thing. This supports evidence discussed on p. 45.

The work with the problem-solving scale is still in its infancy and the scale is still being refined. For example, a seventh factor, labelled *support seeking* in problem situations, has been added to the scale. The evidence in addition to the approach–avoidance work discussed above is that the person who has a strong sense of control, is more creative and confident, and who does not tend to feel helpless is better at coping with stress. For the support-seeking factor, again there is conflicting evidence suggesting that a very high tendency to seek support in problem situations is not a very effective coping strategy and may reflect a tendency to avoid dealing with problems. A tendency not to seek support at all is equally detrimental.

What all this evidence indicates is that the way in which people think about problems (their problem-solving style) is important in determining whether or not they will cope effectively with life stress. Those who have a generally positive problem-solving style are more resistant to stress and as a consequence are less likely to develop psychological or physical health problems. In addition, those who have developed problems in living can benefit from interventions which focus on improving their general problem-solving style. This applies to both physical and mental health problems and to behavioural problems across the developmental range.

The role of motivation

Lazarus and Folkman (1984) identify commitments as central to cognitive appraisal in the stress process and go on to define commitments in terms of the goals individuals value in life. Commitments and goal value have been explored in psychology under the banner of achievement strivings or achievement motivation. It is not a new concept. William James (1890) described achievement strivings as central to the psychology of the individual. Murray (1938) argued in his theory of personality that achievement motivation was one of the major needs, and introduced the abbreviation nAch. Gordon Allport also saw this striving to achieve as playing a central role in personality, something which he called 'becoming' and proposed as an essential state for the healthy personality (Allport, 1955).

In the 1950s nAch was explored by McClelland and his colleagues using projective techniques (McClelland et al., 1953). They identified characteristics of individuals which reflected more or less of an intrinsic competence motivation. Over the years their approach has generated a vast amount of data linking nAch with a wide range of outcomes such as risk preference (Atkinson, 1957), performance (Cooper, 1983), entrepreneurship (McClelland, 1965) and social adjustment (Veroff, 1982). The work generated by this approach has tended to focus on work-related variables and task-related activities, and has tended not to engage with the link between nAch and psychological well-being suggested in the work of the earlier theorists cited above. Some of the work does suggest a relationship between nAch and health (Veroff, 1982; McClelland, 1979). Other studies have shown nAch to be related to self-esteem (Tanwar and Sethi, 1986), to emotional maturity (Verma, 1986), to delinquency (Thilagaraj, 1984) and anxiety in a cross-cultural sample (Ray, 1990). In summary, it appears that those who have a strong tendency to strive to achieve are also better at coping with life stress than their less striving peers.

The early work on nAch evolved within the context of personality theory and tended to be based on the assumption that nAch is a stable personality trait. The growth in cognitive perspectives over recent years has tended to question that assumption. The role of cognitions in nAch is acknowledged by McClelland (1985) in his conclusion that the expression of nAch may be observed only when the person perceives themselves as having some control over outcomes. This conclusion, drawn from a wide range of work on the relationship between nAch and performance, is echoed in the work of Weiner (1985, 1986) on the relationship between nAch and attributional style. The influence of cognitive theories has been to suggest that nAch is better treated as a more flexible cognitive style which mediates between the environment and behaviour and helps to direct the focus towards a developmental perspective on nAch. The evidence supports a socialisation process approach to nAch (Eccles, 1983; Hetherington et al., 1983). Boykin (1983) identifies the effect of psychological experience on goal expectancies, and in a longitudinal study Cassidy and Lynn (1991) show that socio-economic and family background are predictive of nAch. Bal (1988) showed that children of employed mothers scored higher on nAch than children of unemployed mothers. Carr and Mednick (1988) showed that non-traditional sex role training leads to higher nAch for girls while traditional sex role training leads to higher nAch for boys. Galejis et al. (1987) found that parents' achievements and social position were predictive of the nAch of their offspring. Essentially, one is not born with a strong tendency to strive but instead one acquires this tendency through the learning process. Achievement motivation is sensitive to context and subject to change as a consequence of time and situation.

The relationship between nAch and psychological health was brought to the fore again by Diener (1984) and Emmons (1986). Just as with the earlier theorists, both Diener and Emmons saw personal striving to attain goals within the social environment as the essence of psychological well-being. The argument, which echoes the notions of James (1890) and Allport's (1955) concept of 'becoming', is that psychological health exists in the striving rather than in the achievement. Striving towards goals involves a sense of optimism or hope and would appear to link the concept of achievement motivation with the optimism–pessimism discussed above. The link with attributional style demonstrated by Weiner provides indirect support for this link since for Weiner the stable–unstable dimension of attributions was the most important. This dimension represents optimism–pessimism. The essence of the achievement motivation–optimism link is perhaps best expressed in the words of Robert Louis Stevenson, 'to travel hopefully is a better thing than to arrive.'

Social support and cognition

After what is probably the most comprehensive programme of research on social support, Sarason *et al.* (1990) came to the conclusion that social support is often best understood as a person variable. However, they do tend to conceive of the person aspect of social support as a personality variable. In a later work, Sarason *et al.* (1994) describe their model of social support as an interactional–cognitive model. We have discussed social support in terms of an external resource in some detail in Chapter 4. Clearly, perception of social support does not develop in an environment devoid of supportive interactions, but ultimately it is the individual's personal construction of support within their phenomic world which is most directly related to their behaviour and experience. This is illustrated clearly in the example of the abused children in Chapter 4 (p. 73). Furthermore, it is supported by a vast body of research which shows that individual differences in stress levels and health are better predicted by subjective (perceived) social support than by objective levels of support obtained from a structural or quantitative analysis (Sarason *et al.*, 1990). It appears that social support most clearly conforms to a person-in-context model, in that it is a function of both person and environment and of the interaction between the two.

Emotional reactivity

The role of anxiety in mental health has been explored from a range of perspectives over the past fifty or so years. Most personality theorists agree that anxiety is a dimension which reliably differentiates people. Eysenck (1957) labelled his first personality factor 'neuroticism' to describe a disposition which he had identified in soldiers who were suffering from what would now be labelled post-traumatic stress disorder (PTSD). Over the years the same concept has been a fundamental part of probably all personality taxonomies. It is generally referred to as trait anxiety, and Spielberger et al. (1970: 6) provide a simple definition: 'relatively stable individual differences in anxiety proneness'.

Currently, many personality theorists support what has become known as the 'big five' model of personality. This is based on the finding that all the major psychometric models of personality can be reduced to five main factors, and in all the twelve different big-five models that have been produced since 1949 trait anxiety is identified (John, 1990). Of the twelve, two describe the dimension as neuroticism (McCrea and Costa, 1985; Conley, 1985), three as emotional stability (Tupes and Christal, 1961; Norman, 1963; Goldberg, 1981), one as emotional instability (DeRaad et al., 1988), one as emotionality (Borgatta, 1964), one as ego strength–anxiety (Digman and Takemoto-Chock, 1981), one as dominant–assured (Botwin and Buss, 1989), one as satisfaction (Field and Millsap, 1989) and one as affect (Peabody and Goldberg, 1989). While there is some debate about the consistency and comparability of measures, it seems the consistency of the findings is remarkable. If one were to draw a common theme from the various descriptors used for trait anxiety it would appear to be emotional reactivity.

Another debate concerns trait versus state anxiety. State anxiety refers to a transient anxiety proneness which is invoked by particular events, for example exams, but which does not reflect the person's general reaction. The state anxious person would tend to be constantly anxious. In many ways the distinction concerns the difference between levels of trait anxiety. People with a high score on trait anxiety appear to react anxiously to all life situations, while the person with a low trait anxiety score tends to react anxiously only in those situations which can generally be objectively defined as anxiety provoking; that is, they are situations which provoke anxiety in most if not all people.

There has also been ongoing debate about the cause of trait anxiety. Eysenck (1967) puts forward a case for biological determinism, suggesting that trait anxiety is directly related to levels of physiological arousal in the central nervous system. He suggests that some people have central nervous systems which are easily aroused and hence have high trait anxiety while those with less easily aroused central nervous systems have low trait anxiety. Eysenck argues that these differences in arousability in the central nervous system are inherited; that is, they are genetically transmitted. While the evidence that anxiety levels and levels of central nervous system arousal are positively correlated is probably indisputable, the direction of effect suggested by Eysenck is very much disputed. Spielberger (1972), for example, argues that differences in trait anxiety are a function of early childhood experiences. Thus we learn to be more or less anxious and our central nervous systems adapt to reflect these differences. Gray (1982), who supports the view that there is a physiological base for anxiety, is critical of the heredity argument. He suggests that the studies which support heredity of anxiety show at best that only 50 per cent of the variance in anxiety is inherited, which leaves at least another 50 per cent unexplained. Clearly, learning plays an important role in this 50 per cent. Michael Eysenck is critical of the view that anxiety is caused by physiological processes on the basis that if this were true, 'those individuals who have especially responsive physiological systems should tend to be rather anxious and stressed in most, or even all, stressful situations, whereas those with unresponsive physiological systems should characteristically experience relatively little anxiety in any situation' (Eysenck, 1988: 434). Eysenck (1988) goes on to argue that anxiety has a number of systems other than the physiological system and that traditional trait anxiety approaches are inadequate because they ignore the role of the cognitive system.

We saw in the discussion of theories of emotion at various points throughout the current and previous chapters that emotions cannot be explained adequately by ignoring cognitions. Eysenck (1988) describes the cognitive system as acting as a gateway to the physiological system and suggests that the vulnerability to clinical anxiety in those high in trait anxiety may be best explained by differences in cognitive functioning. The main aspect of cognitive functioning identified by Eysenck (1988) is the dimension approach–avoidance, which forms the basis of Byrne's (1964) Repression–Sensitisation Scale and is according to Eysenck a measure of trait anxiety. An evaluation of the evidence suggests that sensitisers are high in trait anxiety because they tend to focus information-processing resources on threatening stimuli and are more likely to interpret ambiguous stimuli as threatening. In other words, their cognitive style is of the approach variety, meaning that they are very sensitive to the negative or threatening aspects of their world. Conversely, those low in trait anxiety repress the processing of threatening stimuli and are more likely to focus on the positive or non-threatening aspects of their world. As a consequence, those whose cognitive style leads to high trait anxiety are more vulnerable in the stress process.

One could be forgiven for detecting shades of optimistic versus pessimistic thinking here, and clearly the approach and avoidance dimensions of problem-solving style address a similar process. The essence of the argument put forward by Eysenck (1988) is that the cognitive styles which underlie trait anxiety and which are tapped by measures of trait anxiety determine one's vulnerability or resistance to external demands or stressors. It really does not need research to show that trait anxiety is related to the experience of stress; what is of interest is the cognitive architecture which supports both. The selective processing of information which leads to high or low trait anxiety has been operationally defined by theorists in the experimental tradition as worrying (Eysenck, 1984). The focus on selecting threatening stimuli to attend to, and the bias towards seeing novel or ambiguous stimuli as threatening, leads to a processing of information which reflects the process of worrying. For example, once

I have identified an external event as potentially threatening, I will begin to focus on all its negative aspects. If I have financial problems I may begin to see perfectly innocent behaviour at work as an indication that the boss is not pleased with my work and I may begin to think, 'what if he fires me?' etc. Worrying involves *catastrophising*, a process where everything is viewed negatively and the negative consequences exaggerated. I won't pass the exam, therefore I won't be able to get a job, my girlfriend will leave me, my parents will be disappointed, I will end up on the streets, etc. Worrying and catastrophising depend on the store of information we already have in memory and the way it is organised into schemata, blueprints or constructs in our mind. One might argue that the concept of trait anxiety becomes obsolete and that what is important in understanding vulnerability to stress is the cognitive style. However, inasmuch as this cognitive style is observed as anxiety levels or emotional reactivity and its presence detected by anxiety measures, it would be premature to dispense with its services just yet.

The discussion above suggests that the cognitive style of individuals is of ultimate importance in determining their vulnerability and resistance to stress. We have seen that while there is a great deal of evidence to back each perspective or cognitive style, they are best considered as contributory rather than competing explanations for stress outcomes and that there is a great deal of commonality across styles. At the moment there is no model which addresses this need for integration and clarification of overlap. Before going on to try to build such an integrative model we need to consider the behavioural outcomes of the stress process.

Behavioural outcomes: coping and lifestyles

The preceding discussion clearly shows that stress can have an impact on physical and mental health. This impact is mediated by the individual's coping strategies, which are arguably predicated on their cognitive style. Thus a person who has an approach style will tend to use approach as a strategy. Coping behaviours are largely reflected in the lifestyles of individuals and we will briefly review the evidence on coping behaviours and then look at lifestyles.

The things we do to try to deal with external demands or stressors are intricately linked to the ways we appraise or perceive the event. The most obvious case is that where we perceive that an event is controllable, we will direct our behaviour towards controlling it. For example, when faced with a work demand, we may feel we have control over whether or not we actually accept it and may say no, thus establishing control. Alternatively, we may organise or structure the task into manageable proportions. In fact, definitions of coping reflect its cognitive–behavioural nature. For example, coping is 'the person's cognitive and behavioural efforts to manage (reduce, minimise, master, or tolerate) the internal and external demands of the person–environment transaction that is appraised as taxing or exceeding the resources of the person' (Folkman *et al.*, 1986: 572). A number of researchers have addressed the issue of coping strategies by trying to identify the basic dimensions involved using self-report measures. One could argue that what they identified were the dimensions of coping style or problem-solving style. The most widely used measure is the Ways of Coping Questionnaire (Folkman and Lazarus, 1988) which measures eight coping strategies: *confrontative coping, distancing, self-controlling, seeking social support, accepting responsibility, escape–avoidance, planful problem-solving* and *positive reappraisal*. Endler and Parker (1990) came up with three dimensions: *task-oriented coping, emotion-oriented coping* and *avoidance-oriented coping*. Amirkhan (1990) also came up with three dimensions but labelled them *problem-solving, seeking social support* and *avoidance*. Heppner and Petersen (1982) moved away from coping to talking of problem-solving self-appraisal (basically problem-solving style) and came up with three dimensions labelled *problem-solving control, problem-solving confidence* and *approach–avoidance style*. Clearly, what this sort of research produces are dimensions of cognitive style regarding coping, which can be better considered as problem-solving styles. The six dimensions of problem-solving style discussed on p. 116 (Cassidy and Long, 1996) with the addition of the support-seeking factor would seem to subsume the dimensions of coping style listed above, with perhaps the exception of Folkman and Lazarus's (1988) positive reappraisal.

Reviewing the literature on coping, Lazarus (1993) concludes that coping is complex, depends on whether we perceive that something can be done, is generally consistent across genders, and acts as a powerful mediator of emotional outcomes. Some coping strategies are consistent from situation to situation while others depend on the current context, and the effectiveness of a coping strategy depends on the situation, the person and the outcome we are considering. Hence what might produce a good health outcome might not necessarily produce a good emotional outcome. Giving up smoking is likely to produce better health but may not make us happier (at least in the short term). What seems clear is that the coping behaviour adopted depends on our cognitive appraisal and our cognitive style in stressful contexts. Another approach to coping is to focus on lifestyles as an indicator of particular coping strategies.

Lifestyles and stress

There are many ways in which stress impacts on physical and mental health, as we have seen, and important among these are the health-enhancing or health threatening-behaviours people engage in, in other words their lifestyle. Changes in lifestyle reflect attempts to cope with one's world. There are a number of obvious ways in which the experience of stress influences behaviour, which in turn impacts on the stress process. Stress may influence interpersonal behaviour and relationships and may reduce social support. For example, a worker in a high-stress job may find themselves rowing with their family or friends to the extent that relationships break down, thus taking away one of the major resources in dealing with stress, i.e. social support. Stress may lead to an individual taking longer to seek help, either through negative coping strategies such as alcohol or drug misuse, or simply through withdrawal. So instead of talking to someone about the mounting problems at work I may stop off at the pub every evening after work. Moreover, stress may influence the response to illness so that recovery is inhibited because of non-adherence to medical regimes or through unhealthy lifestyles. Even though I have elevated blood pressure I may continue to drink too much alcohol or neglect the exercise that I have been advised to take.

One of the biggest problems facing health professionals is the unhealthy lifestyles engaged in by the majority of people. Any text on health psychology will cover the range of problem lifestyle factors that endanger health: smoking, alcohol and drug abuse, overeating, lack of exercise, engaging in unprotected sex, and risk-taking in general. The evidence is that engaging in things like alcohol and drug abuse, smoking and taking risks is clearly related to elevated levels of stress and that conversely engaging in exercise and eating a healthy diet help people to cope with stress. In addition, for many people unhealthy lifestyles become an additional source of stress. For example, excess alcohol consumption is related to aggression, accidents and the breakdown of relationships. Even healthy lifestyles can become a source of stress to some extent; for example, some people become obsessive about exercise. One might argue that obsession with or addiction to exercise is taking things too far and is therefore not healthy, but you can see the fine line that distinguishes between healthy and unhealthy. The exercise addict may be physically healthy but mentally less so.

Summary

We have reviewed a substantial amount of evidence which attests to the importance of cognitive appraisal or cognitive style in mediating the stress process. It is hoped the reader will agree that this cognitive style approach better captures the role of the person in the stress process than the traditional personality trait perspective. While there is strong support for all of the variables discussed, no one variable is an outright winner in the stress stakes. Each variable contributes to an explanation of psychological mediation of stress. In addition, there appears to be quite a large amount of overlap or commonality across variables. What we have is a set of building blocks which together form the framework for a cognitive model of the stress process.

What is missing is a plan of how the blocks fit together and whether or not all the blocks are necessary. It may well be that some blocks can be discarded altogether, while others need to be pared of extraneous material. Researchers have gone some way in linking some variables, but a lot is yet to be done. In the next chapter we will explore ways in which an integration of material might be pursued, what such an integration might look like, and the principles that might guide us in the search for a more comprehensive explanatory framework.

Further reading

This area is even more diverse than those covered in previous chapters and, as I have suggested, each perspective tends to have its own literature. The reader who is interested in specific areas should follow up some of the references provided. For a discussion of the sort of thinking which underpins the approach advocated it would be useful to read:

Lazarus, R. S. (1993). From psychological stress to the emotions: a history of changing outlooks. *Annual Review of Psychology*, 44, 1–21.

Chapter 7

An integrative model for stress research

W^{E} HAVE DISCUSSED THE various components of a person-in-context model of stress and it now behoves us to draw together these strands into an overall picture of the process. We have looked at the external world (the context) in terms of demands imposed upon the person (stressors) and in terms of the resources it provides which may enhance the coping process. We have considered the person aspect in terms of the biological process involved and in terms of the psychological process. The latter we have divided into personality perspectives and the more recent cognitive style approach.

Most textbooks on stress, for the purposes of explanation, present diagrams of the stress process supported by the evidence. While clearly one does not believe that behaviour and experience occur in such a rational or categorical fashion, the various components are identifiable. In the real world the relationship between the components is complex, dynamic and interdependent, and often operates below the level of conscious awareness. Yet if, as is the ultimate aim of psychology, we want to improve the lot of human beings, we do need practical guidelines. The flow charts or diagrams are no more than that. A typical model is the one shown as Figure 5, taken from Rutter *et al.* (1993). In this model, external pressures or demands are identified in terms of examples such as employment, social class, and so on, while cognitive dispositions are not exemplified. In many ways this is a limitation of most previous models; that is, they tend not to explicate the fact that cognitive dispositions are not a single dimension. This is a consequence of the tendency for each cognitive perspective to be pursued in a separate literature and the variables presented as competing rather than contributory. Yet it is clear that interaction and overlap exist between variables; take for example the argument in the previous chapter that attributional style can be largely subsumed under the two themes control and optimism.

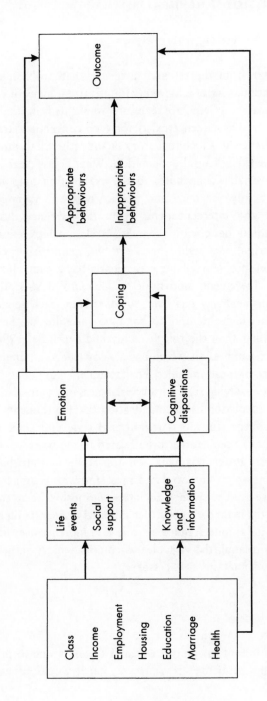

FIGURE 5 The mediators of health

Source: Rutter et al. (1993)

Relationship between cognitive styles

It seems clear from the research evidence that problem-solving style, attributional style, achievement motivation, locus of control and emotional reactivity are causally implicated in the stress process. Given that evidence exists for each conceptual strand, it is obvious that each is a contributory factor rather than providing a single, over-riding causal explanation. What is less clear is how much each variable contributes to the explanation of psychological vulnerability/resistance and in fact how the variables are inter-related and interdependent. From the evidence discussed above it should be obvious that inter-relationships exist. For example, attributional style reflects the two main themes control and optimism, problem-solving style clearly has a control component, and achievement motivation is also linked to optimism. However, the tendency has been to investigate each separately, and research which attempts to combine variables has been the exception rather than the rule (Cassidy and Burnside, 1996).

Some research exists which has acknowledged an interaction between some of these variables. For example, Dixon *et al.* (1991) linked problem-solving style with hopelessness and perceived stress levels in the prediction of suicide ideation (having thoughts about suicide) in college students. Attributional style and achievement motivation have been shown to be related in the work of Weiner (1985, 1986). Problem-solving self-appraisal and attributional style were shown to be correlated in a study by Heppner *et al.* (1985). These studies suggest an inter-relationship between variables, yet in the main each construct supports a separate literature. In order to fully understand their role a comprehensive, integrative analysis treating the variables as complementary rather than competing explanations is necessary.

An integrative model

There is insufficient integrative research to allow one to produce a definitive model of the stress process, but it would appear that research in the area is at the stage where a model is required to guide future research if some of the unnecessary noise in the process is to be removed. One possible such model is shown in Figure 6. The model is based on current evidence and suggests a way forward in integrating the research efforts of those interested in the stress phenomenon. The model tries to bring together what is currently known about the stress process in terms of external demands and resources, internal psychological processes and health/illness outcomes.

In terms of external demands there is a need to consider the person's total life context at all levels and across all life domains. This entails a number of aspects:

- Factors that impinge on the person need to be identified across the person's complete current context in terms of home, family, work, travel, social and other life domains. We are unlikely to understand a person's experience of stress if we ignore any aspect of their life. To understand why someone is experiencing stress at work we need to understand the demands of their home, family and social life, their economic circumstances, their problems in commuting, etc., as well as the demands made upon them by their work context.

- Factors within and across life domains need to be considered at all possible levels, including the immediate context, groups that are significant to the person and broader factors in their work organisation, community, society and culture. As we saw from Bronfenbrenner's analysis, the social and physical contexts within which we live are constituted of a range of interdependent systems, none of which operates in isolation, and which contain factors whose influence on us may be direct or indirect. The fact that there are high levels of unemployment may not have a direct impact on me if I am working, but it may make it more difficult for me to change or leave a high-stress job.

- Factors across life domains and at a range of levels need to be considered in an historical or developmental context. If I have just started a new job I may find myself isolated and

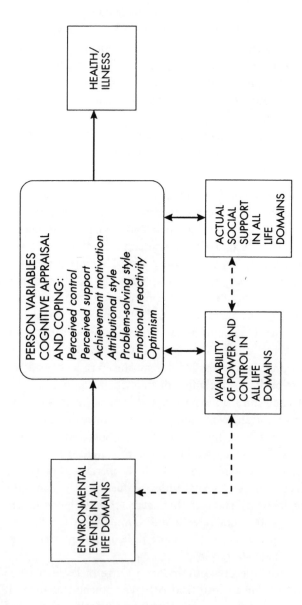

FIGURE 6 An integrative model of the stress process

overwhelmed by job demands while feeling reluctant to argue with my boss. The experienced employee may be able to offset the stress of a similar situation through having support from established friendships, being better able to prioritise tasks, and having the confidence to say no to his or her boss.

In addition, the external world contains resources which enhance one's ability to cope with stress, and these factors need to be considered as well. In particular, we need to assess the support networks, the functions they serve, and the opportunities for control that exist in the person's world. Certainly if we are interested in interventions we need to consider how external resources can be improved.

In terms of psychological processes we need to consider the range of cognitive style factors that have been identified from research. To focus on one factor is likely to lead to a lack of success in intervention. The literature does not allow us to draw strong conclusions about how the different cognitive styles are related or how they interact. One possible model which has perhaps most support to date suggests that the dominant themes are control, optimism and social support. It appears that attributional style, achievement motivation and problem-solving style relate strongly to outcomes of control and optimism. The evidence suggests that the outcome of all three factors is a sense of more or less control, and a sense of hope/optimism or pessimism. Emotional reactivity and problem-solving style relate to social support. Certainly it seems that the way forward in research must involve a clarification of this cognitive structure that underpins appraisal and coping.

Basic principles for future research

Whatever the outcome of future research regarding the validity of the proposed model, research needs to be based on a number of important basic principles. These principles are supported by research evidence and are outlined below.

1   *A person-in-context approach*: This follows Lewin's (1951) famous equation; B = f(P.E), which means that behaviour (B) is a function (f) of the person (P), the environment (E) and the interaction between the two. Thus stress cannot be understood by a summative analysis of person and environment factors alone, but must consider how the person interacts with their world.

2   *A systems perspective:* The systems perspective focuses on the interdependence of parts. In terms of stress this breaks down to a number of levels. First of all, the parts outlined in the model are interdependent, in that change in one part will affect other parts. Hence a change in the environmental demands will effect change in cognitive appraisal and so on. Second, within each part of the model the constituent parts are interdependent. For example, the external environment involves demands and resources in all life domains (e.g. home, work, commuting), and at different levels (e.g. the immediate context, the neighbourhood, society at large). Changes in demands will lead to changes in resources, and changes in one domain or level is likely to produce change in other domains or levels. Similarly, the different aspects of cognitive style operate as parts of an interdependent system. It follows therefore that a complete understanding cannot be attained by focusing exclusively on parts of the process.

3   *A holistic framework:* This suggests that reductionist approaches are limited in their utility and are useful only in the context of a more holistic framework. For example, it is useful to explore problem-solving style in isolation from other aspects of the model only if the aim is to relate the findings back to the overall process. This critique of reductionist approaches is offered even in that most reductionist of sciences, physics. In the words of Stephen Hawking, 'If everything in the universe depends on everything else in a fundamental way, it might be impossible to get close to a full solution by investigating parts of the problem in isolation' (1988: 13).

4 A *dynamic process:* Related to the systems model is the notion that the stress process is a dynamic process where cause and effect are multidirectional rather than unidirectional. Thus it is not simply a matter of identifying a set of stressors, a particular cognitive style and a health outcome, but rather recognising that the health outcome then becomes a causal factor in the process. For example, a person who works in a high-stress job and who has a pessimistic cognitive style is likely to develop stress-related illness. In a unidirectional model an intervention might try to change the demands of the job and help the person become more optimistic. What is missed by this approach is that the illness has now become a source of stress itself. In other words, what is causing stress now is not what produced the stress in the first place.

5 A *developmental perspective:* Very much related to the dynamic view of stress is the recognition that it conforms to a developmental model. This can be considered at least at two levels. In terms of the overall life span, sources of stress, cognitive styles and coping strategies will differ as the person progresses from childhood, through adulthood into old age. Second, the immediate context of the stress process is subject to developmental change, so that what is happening in the early stages of a stressful situation (e.g. beginning to realise that one is in a very stressful job) will differ from later stages (e.g. when one has realised that one's health and relationships are being destroyed by the ongoing stress and poor coping). This reflects the dynamic process outlined above.

6 *Multiple levels of analysis:* Traditionally psychology has focused at the individual level in seeking explanations for behaviour and experience. The five basic perspectives in psychology (behavioural, cognitive, biological, psychodynamic and humanistic) focus on factors either within the person or in their immediate environment. In addition, each has its own level of individual focus; for example, the psychodynamic perspective tends to focus at the depth level

(below the level of conscious awareness) while the cognitive perspective focuses at a more surface level (at the level of conscious processing). Clearly, a complete understanding of the stress process requires a consideration of all the traditional psychological perspectives, and in addition must move beyond the immediate context into realms traditionally inhabited by sociology, anthropology and other disciplines. It must consider the broader social context (community, neighbourhood, society, culture, etc.) and factors at the level of groups, organisations and societies. It is not enough to look at the daily workload, or the personal interactions of a worker, to understand why they feel stressed; it is necessary to consider management attitudes, organisational policies on support, etc. to complete the picture.

7   *Multiple methods:* To accomplish the task of a multiple-level analysis requires a combination of methods. We need to combine quantitative and qualitative methods and to be aware of the ecological validity of our approach. Cialdini's (1980) *full-cycle model* is to be preferred in that we need to test our findings from one method through the use of other methods in other contexts. Hence from observations made in the real world we may formulate questions that can be tested using controlled experimental techniques, but we must then test our findings from these approaches in real-world settings through perhaps surveys, interviews or more interactional methodologies.

8   *The role of meaning:* The problem with using multiple levels of analysis is that one may be tempted to ask if we are in danger of becoming sociologists or anthropologists or something other than psychologists. One answer to that might be that that may not be such a bad thing since interdisciplinary work is necessary (see below). An alternative answer is to see if the end process of a multiple-level approach can fit with what we see psychology to be. The traditional distinction between psychology and other social sciences has been that psychology is exclusively the study of behaviour and experience, and indeed the multiple-level perspective can

easily maintain that distinction. While multiple-level factors are included in the analysis, it is ultimately in the way people appraise, interpret and give meaning to these events that they have their impact on behaviour and experience. It is a core principle of the psychological approach to stress that it is the meaning of an event for an individual that is its most important defining factor.

9   *Interdisciplinary work:* While the psychological perspective is distinct from that of other disciplines, the issue of stress touches on so many disciplines from medicine to social policy that psychologists interested in stress ignore them at their peril. In applied fields where explanations and interventions must occur in real contexts the artificial boundaries of academia become blurred and often disappear.

10 *The person as active, not passive:* Very much related to the issue of meaning is the assumption that the person is active and not passive in the stress process. People act on their world in order to change it through their coping strategies.

11 *Personal agency:* The active processing of information and giving meaning to experience raises the issue of personal agency or free will. While there is insufficient space here to engage with the free will–determinism debate, it is important that we address the question of what sort of person we see when we investigate the stress process. It would appear that insomuch as we focus on the active attribution of meaning and the ability of the person to reflect on their own experience, we are according them at least a modicum of free will or personal agency in an otherwise largely determined world.

The research evidence we have considered in this text has not always conformed to the principles outlined above. Clearly, much of the research has been reductionist, relying on a single method and focusing on just one level. Quantitative and qualitative methods have very seldom been used together. Studies have looked at person variables and environmental factors separately. However, there is some evidence that theorists have begun to move away from traditional approaches and that while what has been produced has been useful, the limitations of previous research can be identified in terms of several if not all of the above principles. The model presented and the utilising of the eleven principles outlined would seem to be a useful way forward in stress research.

Summary

In this chapter I have suggested that the literature on stress, while substantial and informative, is currently in need of an integrative model. Because it is such a complex and vast area it has been necessary in the past to explore it in a piecemeal fashion. However, such an approach would appear to have reached the end of its usefulness. It seems sensible at this stage in the evolution of stress research to bring together what has been gleaned from past research in an integrative model to guide future research. We have considered such a model briefly and examined some principles upon which future developments need to build. It is not a case of disparaging what has been done; rather, it is a constructive criticism which can provide a guiding light to the future. It is useful at this stage to finish off our discussion of stress by identifying some specific areas which are indicated and appear promising for the future of the area, and this is the subject matter for the final chapter.

Further reading

In many ways what this chapter attempts goes beyond what has been done previously. Consequently, there are no specific texts or articles that are appropriate. However, the reader might wish at this point to peruse the ideas of the most prolific researcher in the area, i.e. R. S. Lazarus. A good place to start would be:

Lazarus, R. S. and Folkman, S. (1984). *Stress, appraisal and coping*, New York: Springer.

Chapter 8

Future
directions

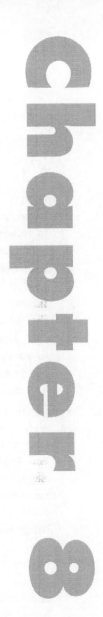

141

OUR DISCUSSION HAS COVERED the main focus of stress research in psychology and culminated in a model which reflects the main findings. It is useful to finish off with a look at where research might go in the future. Researchers have begun to recognise and acknowledge the limitations of past research and it is in addressing what has been neglected or omitted in the past that new developments are likely to occur. Past research, has predominantly drawn on the quantitative research paradigm, and the current advance in qualitative methods provides both a strong case and a means for redressing the balance.

Linked to this are the stirrings of the constructivist approach to stress research. This has implications for moving away from an individual-level focus, and, combined with developments in social cognition, particularly in the area of social identity and social categorisation, provides a means for conceptualising and investigating group- and societal-level factors.

Related to this is the need to recognise and explore the social and physical context of health and illness at a range of levels. Arguably community and environmental psychology provide a useful model for this development. This more comprehensive analysis of context and cognitions must address the developmental nature of the stress process, which requires more longitudinal research.

There is also the issue of stress across life domains and the tendency in the past to focus on single domains as if they were independent of the rest of life, for example work stress. This means considering the interaction and interdependence between domains and recognising changes in the importance of life domains; for example, the growth in importance of leisure.

Finally, there is the growing recognition of the importance of stress and emotional functioning over traditional foci on ability, intelligence and other basic skills. We will look at each of these areas briefly.

Cognition and constructions of reality

In discussing the cognitive appraisal processes and how they are related to behaviour and experience one cannot ignore the similarities with George Kelly's (1955) personal construct theory and with constructionist perspectives in psychology generally, despite the differences in terminology. These approaches are grounded in existential and phenomenological philosophy, a discussion of which is beyond the scope of this text. The essence of Kelly's theory is that there are as many versions of reality as the human mind is capable of conceiving. As a result of different past experiences, biological differences and so forth, we may all view the same situation but come away with a different story. The different stories we develop, or the different ways in which we construct reality to use the terminology, will be stored as part of our internal view or mental map of the world. These are, in different terms, our personal constructions of reality or our cognitive appraisals of the situation.

Thus we will behave in different ways. Two people working in the same stressful job may differ, so that one spends his evenings drinking alcohol while the other goes for a 10-mile run. For every experience in the world we develop a mental map or personal construct or a cognitive appraisal. While constructions of reality do not occur in the absence of external events, they rework the external events into personal meanings which ultimately determine the individual differences in behaviour and experience that we observe.

It is important to recognise the similarity in thinking between current advocates of the cognitive appraisal approach to stress and the constructivists, particularly George Kelly, who was a clinical psychologist and explained psychological problems in terms of the inability to modify one's construct system in response to external events. In essence, psychological problems occurred as a result of the cognitive appraisal of life events.

Constructionist grounded theory

The discussion of constructivist perspectives is important in the context of the development of critical psychology. Smith *et al.* (1995a, b) discuss a qualitative alternative to the traditional quantitative approach to psychology in terms of constructivist-grounded theory. In essence this presents an approach in which

> the analysis is not driven by prior theory, but instead seeks to adopt a 'bottom-up' approach, in which the data themselves suggest theoretical insights, and these are developed through an iterative process which ultimately leads to theory which is firmly grounded in, and derived from, human experience.
>
> (Smith *et al.*, 1995a: 3)

Thus theory is developed from data grounded in personal constructions of reality or cognitive appraisals of the situation. It has been the case generally that quantitative and qualitative perspectives have been seen as providing alternative and competing explanations and have been addressed in separate literature. However, there is a good case for integrating the two perspectives, certainly in the stress literature.

Traditionally, constructivist perspectives, and Kelly's work in particular, have focused on the essential individuality of human behaviour, an ideographic stance. In other words, it is suggested that every individual is different. In addition to taking an idiographic stance, theorists in this tradition have been fervent followers of the hermeneutic approach, i.e. the belief in the central role of meaning in behaviour and experience – hence Kelly's famous adage, 'If you really want to know how someone feels, ask them; they may actually tell you' (1955). Moscovici (1984), a French psychologist, suggests that a focus on meaning does not necessarily require an idiographic stance, and that there can be a great deal of common or shared meaning. This is the basis of his *social representation theory* (SRT). SRT holds that inasmuch as people share a social context they will construct shared meanings (constructions of reality) or, in alternative terms, shared cognitive appraisals and cognitive maps. Thus while still placing importance on personal meaning we can account for the similarities between people as well as their differences.

Social cognition

Social identity theory (Tajfel and Turner, 1979) or social categorisation theory (Turner, 1985) also reaches similar conclusions. (The latter is a reformulation of the former). According to this perspective, when we appraise our world we organise it into categories in our minds. When we do this with our social world we engage in what is called social categorisation. Using these categories in our mind we compare and contrast the members of different categories. In social categorisation we will have put ourselves into some of the categories, for example, I might categorise my self in terms of male, university lecturer, father, etc. The way we categorise events is an important part of the cognitive appraisal process, which has not been really explored from this perspective. Previous social cognition research which has been incorporated into explanations for stress has tended to focus on the individual level, for example attribution theory. There is a need to incorporate the group- and societal-level analysis provided by social identity and social representation theory into a more comprehensive analysis of the stress process.

Stress as discourse

An important aspect of the social identity and social representation approaches is that they rely heavily on combining qualitative and quantitative paradigms and using a range of different research methods. For example, social identity has been approached using experimental methods, questionnaires, interviews and discourse analytic techniques. While there has been a strong resistance among traditional researchers to relinquishing the reductionist experimental paradigm, a growing number of qualitative researchers who align themselves with what has been labelled *critical psychology* (see Smith *et al.*, 1995b) have moved to the alternative extreme. These theorists argue that behaviour and experience are constructed through discourse and cannot be understood by any other means.

While I can only raise the issue here, it is important to acknowledge the critique of stress from the discourse analytic perspective (Radley, 1994). The essence of this critique is that stress is a mythology created by both researchers and lay persons alike to help to explain the relationship between external events and health or illness. It is a social representation (a shared rhetoric) constructed by people who share a common social context. In this sense it could be seen as an historical phenomenon which will eventually pass. Theorists do suggest that external events are related to illness, but would argue that this is not in a causal manner.

This seems to fly in the face of the psychological distress experienced by those whose contexts impose extreme demands upon them. The critique hinges around the term 'stress' and the myriad of connotations that have become attached to it. Clearly there is a need to include a qualitative aspect in the research and to include an analysis of the social representations of social and cultural factors at higher levels. In addition, we do need to be wary of what we mean by stress. However, it is difficult to see how discarding the term would improve our understanding of health and illness.

Social constructions and stress

The importance of the social representation approach is that it allows us to conceptualise how people come to have common perceptions within a shared social context – for example, how people working within one organisation come to a sense of the shared values, etc., which is often described as the organisational culture. In a similar way people in a community come to a shared representation of the community – for example, the sense of community itself. From both environmental psychology and community psychology the sense of community is recognised as a central aspect of social support and coping with stress (Orford, 1992; Halpern, 1995; Cassidy, 1997).

Culture and stress

The role of societal-level factors in the stress process is evidenced by cultural differences in stress levels and coping. In the literature on Type A behaviour and stress discussed in Chapter 5, a study of Hawaiian men of Japanese descent did not support the job stress–heart disease link and in fact found that the trend was reversed, though not significantly so (Reed et al., 1989). This suggests that for this group high-stress work had an overall positive effect on health. Other studies have found cultural differences in diseases that have been strongly linked to stress. For example, Bond (1991) found much higher rates of death from myocardial infarctions (heart disease) in cultures which valued reputation (broadly speaking, Western societies) more than morality (Eastern cultures such as Chinese). There is also evidence of cultural differences in attributional styles and values generally (Smith and Bond, 1993). What this seems to suggest is that as well as differences in economic advantage there may be important differences in cognitive appraisal and coping processes across cultures which need to be explored.

Developmental aspects

The stress process is clearly developmentally grounded in both the long and the short term, and the only way to understand what is really going on over time is to use longitudinal methods. For a variety of reasons researchers in the stress arena have not engaged with longitudinal analysis. One could argue that the reductionist approaches that have exemplified stress research previously preclude longitudinal study and that useful longitudinal research cannot be carried out in the absence of a comprehensive integrative model. Up until now research has been identifying the various aspects of the model. The sorts of questions one might ask concern when the cognitive styles that make one vulnerable or resistant to stress are laid down and what factors in the development of an individual determine these differences in cognitive style. Answering such questions allows one to think about prevention. There is some evidence that early experiences of support and success lead to later tendencies to perceive support and control. In addition, the work on attachment bonding in childhood suggests a strong link with emotional development, but the link with the development of cognitive styles relevant to stress has not really been explored. Exploring the developmental aspect of the stress process using longitudinal methods seems to be indicated as a necessary future development.

Leisure, a neglected life domain

In discussion of life domains we tend generally to think of home and work as being the two most important ones, with others such as commuting emerging for attention more recently. This is, however, a limited view of the life of most people, and one area that is becoming increasingly important is the area of leisure. In many societies leisure is defined in terms of the absence of other preoccupations, particularly work, rather than as an activity in its own right. Yet very clearly unemployment is not leisure. In fact, leisure is often considered the prerogative and just entitlement of the employed.

It appears that when people are asked to define leisure the most common denominator that emerges is the concept of autonomy or freedom of choice (Argyle, 1992). Leisure is generally associated with positive mental health, but the growth in the importance of leisure time in affluent societies and the ever-expanding leisure industry brings with it important consequences for stress research.

First of all, the number of people trying to access leisure facilities at particular times of the year (public holidays, vacation periods) has imposed a demand on transportation systems (road, rail and air) which seems to be outstripping capacity. Public holiday traffic jams, queues for rides at leisure parks, chaos at airports when flights are delayed, and so on are becoming part of our everyday lives. Yet people seem unwilling or unable to alter their behaviour; thus despite awareness of public holiday traffic jams people continue to use the roads (see Cassidy, 1997 for a discussion).

Second, for many people, partly because of the factors discussed above, holidays are a major source of stress. It is quite common to hear people say they are glad to be back at work after a period of holiday. People in high-stress jobs often find that during time off work they develop all sorts of illnesses, probably related to reduced immune function.

Third, there is some evidence that active and constructive engagement in leisure activities can help in coping with stress (Cassidy, 1996). It certainly seems that leisure time needs to be included in any effective analysis of life stress.

Social and emotional competence versus IQ

It has always been implicit in psychological writing that emotional and social competence is important in attainment, whether at work or school, and for effective performance in life generally. Yet the application of psychology in school and at work has tended to emphasise the intellectual and academic abilities and competencies. More comprehensive theories of intelligence, such as Gardner's (1985) theory of multiple intelligences, incorporate emotional and social competence.

In addition, recent writers have begun to challenge the status quo; an example is Goleman's (1995) concept of emotional intelligence. Clearly, the cost in human and financial terms of stress-related illnesses, both physical and psychological, warrants that we pay more attention to emotional development.

Experiencing stress is not related to intelligence or IQ. The argument is that the cognitive styles that underpin appraisal and coping develop through learning in the same way that intellectual abilities develop and can be nurtured through the developmental process. It is increasingly part of the education system in Western societies to talk of transferable skills and life skills, yet our definition of these seems to be in terms of work-related skills rather than the abilities necessary to cope with life. Some schools in the USA engage with social and interpersonal skills as part of the process of educational delivery, an example being the Interpersonal and Cognitive Problem-solving training package (Spivack and Shure, 1974). There is evidence that this approach helps children to cope more effectively with transition to new schools, for example. It seems with the growing shift in attention towards emotional development that stress research may be able to play an important role in informing practice.

Summary

In this chapter we have taken some of the issues which have been hinted at in other chapters and explored them a little more fully. These are areas where current research is rather lacking, and pursuing these areas in future is likely to enrich the stress literature. These areas follow on from the basic principles outlined in Chapter 7 and reflect current trends in psychological research generally. We finished off by looking at the potential application of stress research in the educational process alongside the more traditional focus in intellectual development. There is clear evidence from the worlds of work and education that health and happiness tend to correlate positively with performance. Perhaps we need to recognise that all three need to be nurtured conjointly if any one of them is to be enhanced.

Glossary

The first occurrence of each of these terms is high-lighted in bold type in the main text.

constructivist perspective The approach epito-mised by the work of George Kelly and his personal construct theory. It is based on the phenomenological strand in philosophy and holds that the world we experience is the world in our minds which we have con-structed as a result of our interactions and transactions with the external world. It is a world of meanings as well as objects.

expectancy-value models These developed within the field of social cognition and are based on the assumption that an individual's behaviour is the result of an interaction between their expectation that the behaviour will succeed in attaining the goal towards which it is directed, and the value of that goal for the individual. Behaviours with a high expectation of success and which are directed towards a valued goal are more likely to be undertaken. The importance of such models is that if we can measure expectation and value then we can more accurately predict behaviour.

interactionist perspective Inspired by the **person–situation debate** and based on the assumption that behaviour is caused by both person variables, and situational variables and by the interaction between the two.

myocardial infarction The medical name for a heart attack. The condition where blood flow to the heart is restricted for one reason or another.

natural killer (NK) cells The disease-recognising cells of the immune system. They are programmed to recognise cells with tumours or viral infections and to respond by destroying or slowing the progress of such cells, thus allowing other immune mechanisms time to respond.

person-situation debate Highlighted in psychology by the publication in 1968 of a book called *Personality and assessment* written by Walter Mischel. The core theme of the book was an attack on the assumptions of temporal and situational stability of personality traits inherent in traditional personality theory. From a situationist perspective Mischel suggested that personality traits observed in one situation may not be present in a different situation. In addition, any consistency in personality traits across situations or across time are the result of similarities in the situations rather than anything to do with the person. The debate led to the growth in the **interactionist perspective** in the 1970s.

phenomic world The world as experienced by the person. It is the world in our minds which is constructed through interaction with the external world and involves not just events but their meaning.

psychometric approach Based on the definition of individual differences through applying scientific principles to the measurement of hypothetical constructs such as intelligence, personality and motivation. It underpins the field of IQ testing and is typified in the field of personality by the work of R. B. Cattell and H. J. Eysenck.

situationist perspective An approach to explaining human behaviour which focuses on external events. It is based on the behavioural tradition in psychology and became popular during the 1970s as a result of Walter Mischel's critique of traditional personality theory. It argues that behaviour is caused and maintained by the situation in which it occurs.

structural equation modelling A relatively new multivariate statistical procedure used in psychology and related social science disciplines to analyse the relationships between variables in a data set. By combining a number of procedures (particularly factor analysis and regression analysis) which are based on correlational techniques it allows one to test complex relationships between large numbers of independent and dependent variables.

T-helper cells The main focus of the body's response to invasion by disease or viral infection. They respond to invasion by producing chemicals which activate other cells such as the **natural killer cells**. The number of T-helper cells in the immune system is an indication of its effective functioning.

References

Abramson, L. Y., Seligman, M. E. P. and Teasdale, J. D. (1978). Learned helplessness in humans: critique and reformulation. *Journal of Abnormal Psychology*, 87, 49–74.

Ader, R. and Cohen, N. (1993). Psychoneuroimmunology: conditioning and stress. *Annual Review of Psychology*, 44, 53–85.

Adler, N. and Matthews, K. (1994). Health psychology: why do some people get sick and some stay well? *Annual Review of Psychology*, 45, 229–59.

Alloy, L. B., Abramson, L. Y., Metalsky, G. I. and Hartlage, S. (1988). The Hopelessness theory of depression: attributional aspects. *British Journal of Clinical Psychology*, 27, 5–21.

REFERENCES

Allport, G. W. (1955). Becoming: basic considerations for a psychology of personality. New Haven, CT: Yale University Press.

Altman, I. (1975). *The environment and social behaviour: privacy, personal space, territoriality, and crowding.* Monterey, CA: Brooks/Cole.

Amirkhan, J. H. (1990) A factor analytically derived measure of coping: the coping strategy indicator. *Journal of Personality and Social Psychology*, 59, 1066–74.

Anderson, B. L., Kiecolt-Glaser, J. K. and Glaser, R. (1994). A biobehavioural model of cancer, stress and disease course, *American Psychologist*, 49, 389–404.

Antoni, M. H., August, S., LaPerriere *et al.* (1990). Psychological and neuroendocrine measures related to functional immune changes in anticipation of HIV-I serostatus notification. *Psychosomatic Medicine*, 52, 496–510.

Antoni, M. H., Baggett, H. L., Ironson, G. *et al.* (1991). Cognitive–behavioural stress management intervention buffers distress responses and immunologic changes following notification of HIV-I seropositivity. *Journal of Consulting and Clinical Psychology*, 59, 906–15.

Argyle, M. (1992). *The social psychology of everyday life.* London: Routledge.

Aspinwall, L. G. and Taylor, S. E. (1992). Modelling cognitive adaptation: a longitudinal investigation of the impact of individual differences and coping on college adjustment and performance. *Journal of Personality and Social Psychology*, 63, 989–1003.

Atkinson, J. W. (1957). Motivational determinants of risk-taking behaviour. *Psychological Review*, 64, 359–72.

Auerbach, S. M. and Kilmann, P. R. (1977). Crisis intervention: a review of outcome research. *Psychological Bulletin*, 84, 1189–1217.

Avis, N. N., Brambilla, J., Vass, K. and McKinlay, J. B. (1991). The effect of widowhood on health: a prospective analysis from the Massachusetts Women's Health study. *Social Science and Medicine*, 9, 1063–2070.

Bachen, E. A., Manuck, S.B., Cohen, S. *et al.* (1995). Adrenergic blockage ameliorates cellular immune responses to mental stress in humans. *Psychosomatic Medicine.*

Bachrach, P. and Baratz, M. (1962). The two faces of power. *American Political Science Review*, 56, 947–52.

Bal, S. (1988). The effect of mother's employment on achievement motivation of adolescents. *Journal of Personality and Clinical Studies*, 4(1), 81–4.

Bandura, A. (1977). Self-efficacy: toward a unifying theory of behavioural change. *Psychological Review*, 84, 191–215.

Bard, P. (1932). The central representation of the sympathetic system. *Archives of Neurology and Psychiatry*, 22, 230–46.

Beale, N. and Nethercott, S. (1985). Job loss and family morbidity: a study of a factory closure. *Journal of the Royal College of General Practitioners*, 35, 510–14.

Beck, A. T. (1976). *Cognitive therapy and the emotional disorders*. New York: International University Press.

Bennett, P. and Carroll, D. (1989). The assessment of Type A behaviour: a critique. *Psychology and Health*, 3, 183–94.

Benschop, R. J., Nieuwenhuis, E. E. S., Tromp, E. A. M. *et al.* (1994). Effects of b-adrenergic blockade on immunologic and cardiovascular changes induced by mental stress. *Circulation*, 89, 762–9.

Bernard, C. (1961). *An introduction to the study of experimental medicine*. New York: Collier. (Original published 1865)

Bieliauskas, L. A. and Garron, D. C. (1982). Psychological depression and cancer. *General Hospital Psychiatry*, 4, 187–95.

Billings, A. G. and Moos, R. H. (1981). The role of coping responses and social resources in attenuating the stress of life events. *Journal of Behavioural Medicine*, 4, 139–57.

Billings, A. G. and Moos, R. H. (1982). Psychosocial theory and research on depression: an integrative framework and review. *Clinical Psychology Review*, 2, 213–37.

Billings, A. G. and Moos, R. H. (1984). Coping, stress and social resources among adults with unipolar depression. *Journal of Personality and Social Psychology*, 46, 877–91.

Billings, A. G. and Moos, R. H. (1985). Psychosocial stressors, coping and depression. In: E. E. Beckham and W. R. Leber (eds), *Handbook of depression: treatment, assessment and research*. Homewood, IL: Dorsey Press.

Bloom, B. L. (1988). *Health psychology: a psychosocial perspective*. Englewood Cliffs, NJ: Prentice-Hall.

Bluhm, C. (1992). Where otters exist as utters: beauty, love and truth in the postmodern world. *Theory and Psychology*, 2(3), 391–6.

Bond, M. H. (1991). Chinese values and health: a cross-cultural examination. *Psychology and Health*, 5, 137–52.

Borgatta, E. F. (1964). The structure of personality characteristics. *Behavioural Science*, 9, 8–17.

Bortner, R. W. (1969). A short rating scale as a potential measure of pattern A behaviour. *Journal of Chronic Diseases*, 22, 87–91.

Botwin, M. D. and Buss, D. M. (1989). Structure of act-report data: Is the five-factor model of personality recaptured? *Journal of Personality and Social Psychology*, 56, 988–1001.

Bowlby, J. (1951). *Maternal care and mental health*. Geneva: World Health Organisation.

Bowlby, J. (1969). *Attachment and loss*, vol. 1. New York: Basic Books.

Bowlby, J. (1980). *Attachment and loss*, vol. 3. New York: Basic Books.

Boykin, A. W. (1983). The academic performance of Afro-American children. In: J. T. Spence (ed.), *Achievement and achievement motives*. San Francisco: W. H. Freeman.

Bradley, L. A., Young, L. D., Anderson, K. O. *et al.* (1987). Effects of psychological therapy on pain behaviour of rheumatoid arthritis patients: treatment outcome and six month follow-up. *Arthritis Rheumatology*, 30, 1105–14.

Branthwaite, A. and Garcia, S. (1985). Depression in the young unemployed and those on Youth Opportunities Schemes. *British Journal of Medical Psychology*, 58, 67–74.

Branthwaite, A. and Trueman, M. (1989). Explaining the effects of unemployment. In: J. Hartley and A. Branthwaite (eds), *The applied psychologist*. Milton Keynes: Open University Press.

Brewin, C. R. (1985). Depression and causal attributions: what is their relation? *Psychological Bulletin*, 98, 297–309.

Briner, R. (1994). Stress as a trivial concept and a modern myth: some alternative approaches to the stress phenomenon. Paper presented to the Annual Conference of the British Psychological Society, Brighton.

Bronfenbrenner, U. (1979). *The ecology of human development: experiments by nature and design*. Cambridge, MA: Harvard University Press.

Broome, A. K. (1989). *Health psychology: processes and applications*. London: Chapman and Hall.

Brown, G. W. (1989). Life events and measurement. In: G. W. Brown and T. O. Harris (eds), *Life events and illness*. London: Unwin.

Brown, G. W. and Birley, J. L. T. (1968). Crises and life changes and the onset of schizophrenia. *Journal of Health and Social Behaviour*, 9, 203–214.

Brown, G. W. and Harris T. O. (1978). *Social origins of depression: a study of psychiatric disorder in women*. London: Tavistock.

Brown, G. W. and Harris T. O. (1989). *Life events and illness*. London: Unwin.

Burns, J. W. and Katkin, E. S. (1991). Hostility and the coronary prone personality. In: H. S. Friedman (ed.), *Hostility, coping and health*. Washington, DC: American Psychological Association.

Byrne, D. (1964). Repression–sensitisation as a dimension of personality. In: B. A. Maher (ed.), *Progress in experimental personality research*. New York: Academic Press.

Cannon, W. B. (1929). *Bodily changes in pain, hunger, fear, and rage*, 2nd edn. New York: Appleton.

Cannon, W. B. (1932). *The wisdom of the body*. New York: Norton.

Carr, P. G. and Mednick, M. T. (1988). Sex-role socialisation and the development of achievement motivation in Black pre-school children. *Sex Roles*, 18(3–4), 169–80.

Carroll, D. (1992). *Health psychology: stress, behaviour and disease*. London: Falmer.

Carver, C. S. and Scheier, M. F. (1981). *Attention and self-regulation: a control-theory approach to human behaviour*. New York: Springer-Verlag.

Cassel, J. (1976). The contribution of the social environment to host resistance. *American Journal of Epidemiology*, 104, 107–113.

Cassidy, T. (1992). Commuting-related stress: consequences and implications. *Employee Counselling Today*, 4(2), 15–21.

Cassidy, T. (1994). Current psychological perspectives on stress: a brief guided tour. *Management Bibliographies and Reviews*, 29(3).

Cassidy, T. (1996). All work and no play: An empirical analysis of the relationship between leisure and health. *Counselling Psychology Quarterly*, 9(1), 77–90.

Cassidy, T. (1997). Environmental psychology: behaviour and experience in context. Hove: Psychology Press.

Cassidy, T. and Burnside, E. (1996). Cognitive appraisal, vulnerability and coping: an integrative analysis of appraisal and coping mechanisms. *Counselling Psychology Quarterly*, 9(3), 261–79.

Cassidy, T. and Dhillon, R. (1997). Type A behaviour, problem-solving style and health in male and female managers. *British Journal of Health Psychology*, 2, 217–27.

Cassidy, T. and Long, C. (1996). Problem-solving style, stress and psychological illness: development of a multifactorial measure. *British Journal of Clinical Psychology*, 35, 265–77.

Cassidy, T. and Lynn, R. (1991). Achievement motivation, educational attainment, cycles of disadvantage and social competence. *British Journal of Educational Psychology*, 61, 1–12.

Cassidy, T. and Newport, S. (1997). Family factors in the development of achievement motivation. Paper presented to the British Psychological Society London Conference, December.

Cialdini, R. B. (1980). Full cycle social psychology. In: L. Bickman (ed.), *Applied Social Psychology Annual*, 1. Beverly Hills, CA: Sage.

Cobb, S. (1976). Social support as a moderator of life stress. *Psychosomatic Medicine*, 38, 300–14.

Cohen, E. L. and Work, W. C (1988). Resilient children, psychological wellness and primary prevention. *American Journal of Community Psychology*, 16, 591–607.

Cohen, J. B. and Reed, D. (1985). The type A behaviour pattern and coronary heart disease among Japanese men in Hawaii. *Journal of Behavioural Medicine*, 8, 343–52.

Cohen, S. and Herbert, T. B. (1996) Health psychology: psychological factors and physical disease from the perspective of human psychoneuroimmunology. *Annual Review of Psychology*, 47, 113–42.

Cohen, S. and Manuck, S. B. (1995). Stress, reactivity and disease. *Psychosomatic Medicine*.

Cohen, S. and Wills, T. (1985). Stress, social support and the buffering hypothesis. *Psychological Bulletin*, 98, 310–57.

Cohen, S., Tyrell, D. A. J. and Smith, A. P. (1991). Psychological distress and susceptibility to the common cold. *New England Journal of Medicine*, 325, 606–12.

Cohen, S., Tyrell, D. A. J., and Smith, A. P. (1993). Negative life events, perceived stress, negative affect, and susceptibility to the common cold. *Journal of Personality and Social Psychology*, 64, 131–40.

Cohen, S., Doyle, W. J., Skoner, D. P., Fireman, P., Gwaltney, J. M. and Newsom, J. T. (1995a). State and trait negative affect as predictors of objective and subjective symptoms of respiratory viral infections. *Journal of Personality and Social Psychology*, 68, 159–169.

Cohen, S., Kessler, R. C. and Underwood Gordon, L. G. (1995b). Strategies for measuring stress in studies of psychiatric and physical disorders. In: S. Cohen, R. C. Kessler and L.G. Underwood Gordon (eds), *Measuring stress: a guide for health and social scientists*. New York: Oxford University Press.

Conley, J. J. (1985). Longitudinal stability of personality traits: a multi-trait–multimethod–multioccasion analysis. *Journal of Personality and Social Psychology*, 49, 1266–82.

Contrada, R. J., Leventhal, H. and O'Leary, A. (1990). Personality and health. In: L. A. Pervin (ed.), *Handbook of personality: theory and research*. New York: Guilford Press.

Cooper, C. L., Cooper, R. D. and Eaker, L. H. (1988). *Living with stress*. London: Penguin Books.

Cooper, W. H. (1983). An achievement motivation nomological network. *Journal of Personality and Social Psychology*, 44, 841–61.

Costa, G., Pickup, L. and Di-Martino, V. (1988). A further stress factor for working people: evidence from the European Community. 1. A review. *International Archives of Occupational and Environmental Health*, 60(5), 371–6.

Deary, I. J., MacLullich, A. M. and Mardon, J. (1991). Reporting of minor physical symptoms and family incidence of hypertension and heart disease: relationships with personality and Type A behaviour. *Personality and Individual Differences*, 12, 747–51.

DeLongis, A., Coyne, J. C., Dakof, G. *et al.* (1982). Relationship of daily hassles, uplifts, and major life events to health status. *Health Psychology*, 1, 119–36.

Denham, S. A. and Almeida, M. C. (1987). Children's social problem-solving skills, behavioural adjustment, and interventions: a meta-analysis evaluating theory and practice. *Journal of Applied Development Psychology*, 8, 391–401.

DeRaad, B., Mulder, E., Kloosterman, K. and Hofstee, W. K. (1988). Personality descriptive verbs. *European Journal of Personality*, 2, 81–96.

Diener, E. (1984). Subjective well-being. *Psychological Bulletin*, 95(3), 542–75.

Digman, J. M. and Takemoto-Chock, N. K. (1981). Factors in the natural language of personality: re-analysis and comparison of six major studies. *Multivariate Behavioural Research*, 16, 149–70.

Dixon, W. A., Heppner, P. P. and Anderson, W. P. (1991). Problem-solving appraisal, stress, hopelessness, and suicide ideation in a college population. *Journal of Counseling Psychology*, 38, 51–6.

Dohrenwend, B. S., Krasnoff, L., Askenasy, A. R and Dohrenwend, B. P. (1978). Exemplification of a method for sealing life events: the PERI life events scale. *Journal of Health and Social Behaviour*, 19, 205–29.

Durkheim, K. (1897/1951). *Suicide*. New York: Free Press.

Eccles, J. (1983). Expectancies, values and academic behaviours. In: J. T. Spence (ed.), *Achievement and achievement motives*. San Francisco: W. H. Freeman.

Emmons, R. A. (1986). Personal strivings: an approach to personality and subjective well-being. *Journal of Personality and Social Psychology*, 51(5), 1058–68.

Endler, N. S. and Parker, J. D. A. (1990). Multidimensional assessment of coping: A critical evaluation. *Journal of Personality and Social Psychology*, 58, 844–54.

Epstein, Y. M. (1982). Crowding, stress and human behaviour. In: G. W. Evans (ed.), *Environmental Stress*. New York: Cambridge University Press.

Esterling, B. A., Antoni, M. H., Fletcher, M. A. *et al.* (1994). Emotional disclosure through writing or speaking modulates latent Epstein–Barr virus antibody titiers. *Journal of Consulting and Clinical Psychology*, 62, 130–40.

Evans, P., Clow, A. and Hucklebridge, F. (1997). Stress and the immune system. *The Psychologist*, 10, 303–307.

Eysenck, H. J. (1957). The dynamics of anxiety and hysteria. London: Routledge and Kegan Paul.

Eysenck, H. J. (1967). *The biological basis of personality*. Springfield, IL: Charles C. Thompson.

Eysenck, H. J. (1985). Personality, cancer and cardiovascular disease: a causal analysis. *Personality and Individual Differences*, 6, 535–56.

Eysenck, M. W. (1984). Anxiety and the worry process. *Bulletin of the Psychonomic Society*, 22, 545–8.

Eysenck, M. W. (1988). Trait anxiety and stress. In: S. Fisher and J. Reason (eds), *Handbook of lifestress, cognition and health*. Chichester: Wiley.

Falk, A., Hanson, B. S., Isaacson, S. and Ostergren, P. (1992). Job strain and mortality in elderly men: social network, support and influence as buffers. *American Journal of Public Health*, 82, 1136–9.

Fawzy, F. I., Fawzy, N. W., Hyun, C. S. *et al.* (1993). Malignant melanoma: effects of an early structured psychiatric intervention, coping, and affective state on recurrence and survival six years later. *Archives of General Psychiatry*, 50, 681–9.

Field, D. and Millsap, R. E. (1989). Personality in advanced old age: continuity or change. Unpublished manuscript, Institute of Human Development, University of California at Berkeley.

Fisher, S. and Reason, J. (eds) (1988). Handbook of life stress, cognition and health. Chichester: Wiley.

Folkman, S. and Lazarus, R. S. (1988). *Manual for the Ways of Coping Questionnaire.* Palo Alto, CA: Consulting Psychologists Press.

Folkman, S., Lazarus, R. S., Gruen, R. J. and DeLongis, A. (1986). Appraisal, coping, health status and psychological symptoms. *Journal of Personality and Social Psychology, 50,* 571–9.

Fox, B. H. (1978). Premorbid psychological factors as related to cancer incidence. *Journal of Behavioural Medicine,* 1, 45–133.

French–Belgian Collaborative Group (1992). Ischaemic heart disease and psychological patterns: prevalence and incidence studies in Belgium and France. *Advances in Cardiology,* 29, 25–31.

Friedman, H., Hall, J. and Harris, M. (1985). Type A, nonverbal expressive style, and health. *Journal of Personality and Social Psychology,* 48, 1299–315.

Friedman, H. S. (1991). Understanding hostility, coping and health. In: H. S. Friedman (ed.), *Hostility, coping and health.* Washington, DC: American Psychological Association.

Friedman, H. S. (1992). *The self-healing personality: why some people achieve health and others succumb to illness.* New York: Academic Press.

Friedman, M. and Rosenman, R. H. (1959). Association of specific overt behaviour pattern with blood and cardiovascular findings: blood cholesterol level, blood clotting time, incidence of arcus senilis, and clinical coronary artery disease. *Journal of the American Medical Association,* 169, 1986.

Friedman, M. and Rosenman, R. (1974). *Type A behaviour and your heart.* New York: Knopf.

Friedman, M. and Ulmer, D. (1984). *Treating Type A behaviour and your heart.* New York: Alfred A. Knopf.

Friedman, M., Thoresen, C. E., Gill, J. J. *et al.* (1986). Alteration of Type A behaviour and its effects on cardiac recurrences in postmyocardial infarction patients: summary of the Recurrent Coronary Prevention Project. *American Heart Journal,* 112, 653–65.

Fuller, T. D., Edwards, J. N., Semsri, S. and Vorakitphokatorn, S. (1993). Housing, stress and physical well-being: evidence from Thailand. *Social Science and Medicine,* 36, 1417–28.

Furnham, A. (1990). The Type A behaviour pattern and the perception of self. *Personality and Individual Differences,* 11, 841–51.

Furnham, A. (1992). *Personality at work.* London: Routledge.

REFERENCES

Galejis, I., King, A. and Hegland, S. M. (1987). Antecedents of achievement motivation in preschool children. *Journal of Genetic Psychology*, 148(3), 333–48.

Gardner, H. (1985). *Frames of mind*. New York: Basic Books.

Glaser, R., Kiecolt-Glaser, J. K., Stout, J. C. *et al.* (1985). Stress-related impairments in cellular immunity. *Psychiatric Research*, 16, 233–9.

Glaser, R., Rice, J., Speicher, C. E. *et al.* (1986). Stress depresses interferon production by leukocytes concomitant with a decrease in natural killer cell activity. *Behavioural Neuroscience*, 100, 675–8.

Glaser, R., Rice, J., Sheridan, J. *et al.* (1987). Stress-related immune suppression: health implications. *Brain, Behaviour and Immunology*, 1, 7–20.

Glaser, R., Pearson, G. R., Jones, J. F. *et al.* (1991). Stress-related activation of Epstein–Barr virus. *Brain, Behaviour and Immunology*, 5, 219–32.

Goffman, E. (1961). *Asylums: essays on the social situation of mental patients and other inmates*. New York: Anchor Books.

Goldberg, L. R. (1981). Language and individual differences: the search for universals in personality lexicons. In: L. Wheeler (ed.), *Review of personality and Social Psychology*, 2, 141–65.

Goleman, D. (1995). *Emotional intelligence: why it can matter more than IQ*. London: Bloomsbury.

Gray, J. A. (1982). *The neuropsychology of anxiety*. Oxford: Clarendon.

Greenberg, J. and Baron, R. A. (1997). *Behavior in organizations*, 6th ed. Englewood Cliffs, NJ: Prentice-Hall.

Greer, S., Morris, T. and Pettingale, K. W. (1979). Psychological response to breast cancer. *Lancet*, ii, 785–7.

Gregory, R. L. (1973). The confounded eye. In: R. L. Gregory and E. H. Gombrich (eds), *Illusions in nature and art*. London: Duckworth.

Grossarth-Maticek, R., Eysenck, H. J. and Vetter, H. (1988). Personality type, smoking habit and their interaction as predictors of cancer and coronary heart disease. *Personality and Individual Differences*, 9, 479–95.

Gulian, E., Matthews, G., Glendon, A. I. *et al.* (1989). Dimensions of driver stress. *Ergonomics*, 32, 585–602.

Haan, M. N. (1988). Job strain and ischaemic heart disease: an epidemiologic study of metal workers. *Annals of Clinical Research*, 20, 143–5.

Halpern, D. (1995). *Mental health and the built environment*. London: Taylor and Francis.

Hanson, B. S., Isaacson, S. O., Janzon, L. and Lindell, S. E. (1989). Social network and social support influence mortality in elderly men. *American Journal of Epidemiology*, 130, 100–11.

Hathaway, S. R. and McKinley, J. C. (1945). *Manual for the Minnesota Multiphasic Personality Inventory*. New York: The Psychological Corporation.

Hawking, S. (1988). *A brief history of time: from Big Bang to black holes*. London: Bantam.

Hayes, N. (1997). *Effective team work*. London: Thompson International Press.

Haynes, S. G., Levine, S., Scotch, N. *et al.* (1978). The relationship of psychosocial factors to coronary heart disease in the Framingham study: 1. Methods and risk factors. *American Journal of Epidemiology*, 107, 362–83.

Hazan, C. and Shaver, P. (1987). Romantic love conceptualised as an attachment process. *Journal of Personality and Social Psychology*, 52, 511–24.

Heider, F. (1958). *The psychology of interpersonal relations*. New York: Wiley.

Heller, K. (1989). The return to community. *American Journal of Community Psychology*, 17, 1–16.

Henley, S. and Furnham, A. (1989). The Type A behaviour pattern and self evaluation. *British Journal of Medical Psychology*, 62, 51–9.

Heppner, P. P. and Petersen, C. H. (1982). The development and implications of a Personal Problem-solving Inventory. *Journal of Counseling Psychology*, 29, 66–75.

Heppner, P. P., Baumgardner, A. and Jackson, J. (1985). The relationship between problem-solving self-appraisal, depression and attributional style: are they related? *Cognitive Therapy and Research*, 9, 105–13.

Heppner, P. P., Kampa, M. and Brunning, L. (1987). The relationship between problem-solving self-appraisal and indices of physical and psychological health. *Cognitive Therapy and Research*, 11, 155–68.

Herbert, T. B., and Cohen, S. (1993). Depression and immunity: a meta-analytic review. *Psychological Bulletin*, 113, 472–86.

Herbert, T. B., Cohen, S., Marsland, A. L. *et al.* (1994). Cardiovascular reactivity and the course of immune response to an acute psychological stressor. *Psychosomatic Medicine*, 56, 337–44.

Herridge, C. F. (1974). Aircraft noise and mental health. *Journal of Psychomotor Research*, 18, 239–43.

REFERENCES

Hetherington, E. M., Camara, K. A. and Featherman, D. L. (1983). Achievement and intellectual functioning of children in one-parent households. In: J. T. Spence (ed.), *Achievement and achievement motives*. San Francisco: W. H. Freeman.

Hibbard, J. and Pope, C. (1993). The quality of social roles as predictors of morbidity and mortality. *Social Science and Medicine*, 36, 217–25.

Hodgkinson, P. E. and Stewart, M. (1991). *Coping with catastrophe*. London: Routledge.

Hollis, J. F., Connett, J. E., Stevens, V. J., and Greenlick, M. R. (1990). Stressful life-events, Type A behaviour, and the prediction of cardiovascular and total mortality over six years. *Journal of Behavioural Medicine*, 13, 263–81.

Holmes, T. H. and Rahe, R. (1967). The Social Readjustment Rating Scale. *Journal of Psychosomatic Research*, 14, 213–18.

Hoon, E. F., Hoon, P. W., Rand, K. H. *et al.* (1991). A psychobehavioural model of genital herpes recurrence. *Journal of Psychosomatic Research*, 35, 25–36.

Jahoda, M. (1987). Unemployed men at work. In: D. Fryer and P. Ullah (eds), *Unemployed People*. Milton Keynes: Open University Press.

Jahoda, M. (1988). Economic recession and mental health: some conceptual issues. *Journal of Social Issues*, 44, 13–24.

Jahoda, M., Lazarsfeld, P. F. and Zeisel, H. (1972). *Marienthal: the sociography of an unemployed community*. London: Tavistock.

James, W. (1884). What is an emotion? *Mind*, 9, 188–205.

James, W. (1890). *The principles of psychology*. New York: Holt.

Jansen, M. A. and Muenz, L. R. (1984). A retrospective study of personality variables associated with fibrocystic disease and breast cancer. *Journal of Psychosomatic Research*, 28, 35–42.

Jenkins, C. D., Zyzanski, S. J. and Rosenman, R. H. (1979). *Jenkins Activity Survey*. New York: The Psychological Corporation.

Jensen, M. R. (1987). Psychobiological factors predicting the course of breast cancer. *Journal of Personality*, 55, 317–42.

John, O. P. (1990) The 'Big Five' factor taxonomy: dimensions of personality in the natural and language and in questionnaires. In: L. A. Pervin (ed.), *Handbook of personality: theory and research*. New York: Guildford Press.

Johnston, D. W., Cook, D. G. and Shaper, A. G. (1987). Type A behaviour and ischaemic heart disease in middle aged British men. *British Medical Journal*, 295, 86–9.

Kahn, R. and Antonucci, T. (1980). Convoys over the life course: attachments, roles and social support. In: P. Baltes and O. Brim (eds), *Lifespan development and behaviour*, vol. 3. New York: Academic Press.

Kamarck, T. W., Manuck, S. B. and Jennings, J. R. (1990). Social support reduces cardiovascular reactivity to psychological challenge: a laboratory model. *Psychosomatic Medicine*, 52, 42–58.

Kanner, A. D., Coyne, J. C., Schaever, C. and Lazarus, R. S. (1981). Comparison of two modes of stress measurement: daily hassles and uplifts versus major life events. *Journal of Behavioural Medicine*, 4, 1–39.

Karasek, R. A., Theorell, T., Schwartz, J. E. *et al.* (1988). Job characteristics in relation to the prevalence of myocardial infarction in the US Health Examination Survey (HES) and the Health and Nutrition Examination Survey (HANES). *American Journal of Public Health*, 78, 910–18.

Kasl, S. and Wells, J. (1985). Social support and health in the middle years: work and the family. In: S. Cohen and S. Syme (eds), *Social Support and Health*. New York: Academic Press.

Kelly, G. (1955). *The psychology of personal constructs*. New York: Norton.

Kemeny, M. E. (1994). Stressful events, psychological responses, and progression of HIV infection. In: R. Glaser and J. Kiecolt-Glaser (eds), *Handbook of Human Stress and Immunity*. New York: Academic Press.

Kemeny, M. E., Weiner, H., Duran, R. *et al.* (1995). Immune system changes following the death of a partner in HIV positive gay men. *Psychosomatic Medicine*.

Kessler, R. C. and McLeod, J. D. (1984). Sex differences in vulnerability to undesirable life events. *American Sociological Review*, 49, 620–31.

Kiecolt-Glaser, J. K., Cacioppo, J. T., Malarkey, W. B. and Glaser, R. (1992). Acute psychological stressors and short-term immune changes: what, why, for whom and to what extent? *Psychosomatic Medicine*, 54, 680–85.

Kissen, D. M. and Eysenck, H. J. (1962). Personality in male lung cancer patients. *Journal of Psychosomatic Research*, 6, 123–7.

Kissen, D. M., Brown, R. I. F. and Kissen, M. (1969). A further report on personality and psychosocial factors in lung cancer. *Annals of the New York Academy of Sciences*, 164, 535–54.

Kobasa, S. C. (1979). Stressful life events, personality and health: an inquiry into hardiness. *Journal of Abnormal and Social Psychology*, 37, 1–11.

REFERENCES

Koffka, K. (1935). *Principles of gestalt psychology.* New York: Harcourt.

Kohler, W. (1940). *Dynamics in psychology.* New York: Liveright.

Lange, C. G. (1885). *The emotions.* Baltimore: Williams and Wilkins.

Lazarus, R. S. (1966). *Psychological stress and the coping process.* New York: McGraw-Hill.

Lazarus, R. S. (1968). Emotions and adaptation: conceptual and empirical relations. In: W. J. Arnold (ed.), *Nebraska Symposium on Motivation.* Lincoln: University of Nebraska Press.

Lazarus, R. S. (1991). Emotion and adaptation. New York: Oxford University Press.

Lazarus, R. S. (1993). From psychological stress to the emotions: a history of changing outlooks. *Annual Review of Psychology,* 44, 1–21.

Lazarus, R. S., Averill, J. R. and Opton, E. M. Jr (1970). Toward a cognitive theory of emotion. In: M. Arnold (ed.), *Feelings and emotions.* New York: Academic Press.

Lazarus, R. S. and Folkman, S. (1984). *Stress, appraisal and coping.* New York: Springer.

Levav, I., Friedlander, Y., Kark, J. D. and Peritz, E. (1988). An epidemiologic study of mortality among bereaved parents. *New England Journal of Medicine,* 319, 457–61.

Levi, L. (1987). Definitions and the conceptual aspects of health in relation to work. In: R. Kalimo, M. A. El-Batawi and C. L. Cooper (eds), *Psychosocial factors at work and their relation to health.* Geneva: World Health Organization.

Lewin, K. (1935). *A dynamic theory of personality.* New York: McGraw-Hill.

Lewin, K. (1951). *Field theory in social science.* New York: Harper.

Ley, P. (1988). *Communicating with patients.* London: Croom Helm.

Locke, S. E., Kraus, L., Leserman, J. *et al.* (1984). Life change stress, psychiatric symptoms, and natural killer cell activity. *Psychosomatic Medicine,* 46, 441–53.

Lumsden, D. P. (1981). Is the concept of 'stress' of any use anymore? In: D. Randall (ed.), *Contributions to primary prevention in mental health: working papers.* Toronto: Office of Canadian Mental Health Association.

McClelland, D. C. (1965). Achievement and entrepreneurship: a longitudinal study. *Journal of Personality and Social Psychology,* 1, 389–92.

McClelland, D. C. (1979). Inhibited power motivation and high blood pressure in men. *Journal of Abnormal Psychology,* 88, 182–90.

McClelland, D. C. (1985). *Human motivation*. Glenview, IL: Scott Foresman.

McClelland, D. C., Atkinson, J. W., Clark, R. A. and Lowell, E. L. (1953). *The achievement motive*. New York: Appleton-Century-Crofts.

McCrea, R. R. and Costa, P. T. (1985). Updating Norman's adequate taxonomy: intelligence and personality dimensions in natural language and in questionnaires. *Journal of Personality and Social Psychology*, 49, 710–20.

McKinnon, W., Weisse, C. S., Reynolds, C. P. *et al.* (1989). Chronic stress, leukocyte subpopulations, and humoral response to latent viruses. *Health Psychology*, 8, 389–402.

McLean, D. E. and Link, B. G. (1994). Unravelling complexity. In: W. R. Avison and I. H. Gotlib (eds), *Stress and mental health: contemporary issues and prospects for the future*. New York: Plenum.

Mann, A. W. and Brennan, P. J. (1987). Type A behaviour score and the incidence of cardiovascular disease: a failure to replicate the claimed association. *Journal of Psychosomatic Research*, 31, 685–92.

Matthews, K. A. and Brunson, B. I. (1979). Allocation of attention and the Type A coronary-prone behaviour pattern. *Journal of Personality and Social Psychology*, 37, 2081–90.

Mischel, W. (1968). *Personality and assessment*. New York: Wiley.

Mischel, W. (1990). Personality dispositions revisited and revised: a view after three decades. In: L. A. Pervin (ed.), *Handbook of personality: theory and research*. New York: Guilford Press.

Monroe, S. M. and Roberts, J. E. (1990). Conceptualising and measuring life stress: Problems, principles, procedure, progress. *Stress Medicine*, 6, 209–16.

Moos, R. H. and Swindle, R. W. (1990). Stressful life circumstances: concepts and measures. *Stress Medicine*, 6, 171–8.

Moscovici, S. (1984). The phenomenon of social representation. In: R. M. Farr and S. Moscovici (eds), *Social Representations*. Cambridge: Cambridge University Press.

Murray, H. A. (1938). *Explorations in personality*. New York: Oxford University Press.

Neisser, U. (1976). *Cognition and reality: principles and implications of cognitive psychology*. San Francisco: W. H. Freeman.

Nezu, A. M. (1987). A problem-solving formulation of depression: a literature review and proposal of a pluralistic model. *Clinical Psychology Review*, 7, 121–44.

Nezu, A. M., Nezu, C. M. and Perri, M. G. (1989). *Problem-solving therapy for depression: theory, research and clinical guidelines.* Chichester: Wiley.

Ng, S. (1980). *The social psychology of power.* London: Academic Press.

Norman, W. T. (1963). Towards an adequate taxonomy of personality attributes: replicated factor structure in peer nomination personality ratings. *Journal of Abnormal and Social Psychology,* 66, 574–83.

Orford, J. (1992). *Community Psychology: Theory and Practice.* Chichester: Wiley.

Orth-Gomer, K., Rosengren, A. and Wilhelmsen, L. (1993). Lack of social support and incidence of coronary heart disease in middle-aged Swedish men. *Psychosomatic Medicine,* 55, 37–43.

Parkes, C. M. (1986). *Bereavement: studies of grief in adult life.* Harmondsworth: Penguin Books.

Parkes, C. M., Benjamin, B. and Fitzgerald, R. G. (1969). Broken heart: a statistical study of increased mortality among widowers. *British Medical Journal,* 1, 740–3.

Peabody, D. and Goldberg, L. (1989) Some determinants of factor structures from personality trait descriptors. *Journal of Personality and Social Psychology,* 57, 552–67.

Pearlin, L. I. (1989). The sociological study of stress. *Journal of Health and Social Behaviour,* 30, 241–56.

Pearlin, L. I., Lieberman, M. A., Menaghan, E. G. and Mullan, J. T. (1981). The stress process. *Journal of Health and Social Behaviour,* 22, 337–56.

Persky, V. W., Kempthorne-Rawson, J. and Shekelle, R. B. (1987). Personality and risk of cancer: 20-year follow-up of the Western Electric Study. *Psychosomatic Medicine,* 49, 435–49.

Phillips, J., Freedman, S., Ivancevich, J. and Mateson, M. (1990). Type A behaviour, self appraisals, and goal setting: a framework for future research. *Journal of Social Behaviour and Personality,* 5, 59–76.

Price, V. (1982). *Type A behaviour pattern: a model for research and practice.* London: Academic Press.

Radley, A. (1994). *Making sense of illness.* London: Sage.

Rahe, R. H. (1968). Life change measurement as a predictor of illness. *Proceedings of the Royal Society of Medicine,* 61, 124–6.

Ray, J. J. (1990). Some cross-cultural explorations of the relationship between achievement motivation and anxiety. *Personality and Individual Differences,* 11, 91–3.

Reed, D. M., LaCroix, A. Z., Karasek, R. A., Miller, D. and MacLean, C. A. (1989). Occupational strain and the incidence of coronary heart disease. *American Journal of Epidemiology*, 129, 495–502.

Reynolds, P. and Kaplan, G. A. (1990). Social connections and risk for cancer: Prospective evidence from the Alameda County study. *Behavioural Medicine*, 9, 101–10.

Rosengren, A., Tibblin, G. and Wilhelmsen, L. (1991). Self-perceived psychological stress and incidence of coronary artery disease in middle-aged men. *American Journal of Cardiology*, 68, 1171–75.

Rosenman, R. H. (1978). Role of type A pattern in the pathogenesis of ischaemic heart disease and modification for prevention. *Advances in Cardiology*, 25, 34–46.

Rosenman, R. H., Brand, R. J., Jenkins, C. D. *et al.* (1975). Coronary heart disease in the western collaborative heart study: final follow up experience of $8^{1}/_{2}$ years. *Journal of the American Medical Association*, 233, 872–7.

Rotter, J. B. (1966). Generalised expectancies for internal versus external control of reinforcement. *Psychological Monographs*, 80.

Rotton, J. (1990). Stress. In: C. E. Kimble (ed.), *Social psychology: studying human interaction*. Dubuque, IA: Wm C. Brown.

Rutter, D., Quine, L. and Chesham, D. J. (1993). *Social psychological approaches to health*. London: Harvester/Wheatsheaf.

Rutter, M. (1972). *Maternal deprivation reassessed*. Harmondsworth: Penguin.

Rutter, M., Tizard, J., Yule, M. *et al.* (1976). Isle of Wight studies, 1964–1974. *Psychological Medicine*, 6, 313–32.

Sanders, C. (1993). Risk factors in bereavement outcome. In: W. Stroebe, M. S. Stroebe and R. Hansson, (eds), *Handbook of bereavement*. New York: Cambridge University Press.

Sarason, I. G., Johnson, J. H. and Siegel, J. M. (1978). Assessing the impact of life changes: development of the Life Experiences Survey. *Journal of Consulting and Clinical Psychology*, 46, 932–46.

Sarason, I. G., Sarason, B. R., Shearin, E. N. and Pierce, G. R. (1978). A brief measure of social support: practical and theoretical implications. *Journal of Social and Personal Relationships*, 4, 497–510.

Sarason, B. S., Pierce, G. R. and Sarason, I. G. (1990) Social support: the sense of acceptance and the role of relationships. In: B. R. Sarason, I. G. Sarason and G. R. Pierce (eds), *Social support: an interactional perspective*. New York: Wiley.

Sarason, B. S., Pierce, G. R. and Sarason, I. G. (1994). General and specific perceptions of social support. In: W. R. Avison and I. H. Gotlib (eds), *Stress and mental health: contemporary issues and prospects for the future*. New York: Plenum.

Schachter, S. (1971). *Emotion, obesity and crime*. New York: Academic Press.

Schachter, S. and Singer, J. (1962). Cognitive, social and physiological determinants of emotional state. *Psychological Review*, 69, 370–99.

Scheier, M. F. and Carver, C. S. (1985). Optimism, coping and health: assessment and implications of generalised outcome expectancies. *Health Psychology*, 4, 219–47.

Scheier, M. F. and Carver, C. S. (1987). Dispositional optimism and physical well-being: the influence of generalised outcome expectancies on health. *Journal of Personality*, 55, 169–210.

Scheier, M. F. and Carver, C. S. (1992). Effects of optimism on psychological and physical well-being: Theoretical overview and empirical update. *Cognitive Therapy and Research*, 16, 201–28.

Scheier, M. F., Weintraub, J. K. and Carver, C. S. (1986). Coping with stress: divergent strategies of optimists and pessimists. *Journal of Personality and Social Psychology*, 51, 1257–64.

Schneiderman, N., Antoni, M., Ironson, G. *et al.*. (1994). HIV-1, immunity, and behaviour. In: R. Glaser and J. Kiecolt-Glaser (eds), *Handbook of human stress and immunity*. New York: Academic Press.

Seligman, M. E. P. (1975). *Helplessness: on depression, development and death*. San Francisco: Freeman.

Seligman, M. E. P. and Maier, S. F. (1967). Failure to escape traumatic shock. *Journal of Experimental Psychology*, 74, 1–9.

Selye, H. (1956). *The stress of life*. New York: McGraw-Hill.

Sieber, W. J., Rodin, J., Larson, L. *et al.* (1992). Modulation of human natural killer cell activity by exposure to uncontrollable stress. *Brain, Behaviour and Immunology*, 6, 141–56.

Siegel, J. M. (1991). Anger and cardiovascular health. In: H. S. Friedman (ed.), *Hostility, coping and health*. Washington, DC: American Psychological Association.

Siegrist, J., Peter, R., Junge, A. *et al.* (1990). Low status control, high effort at work and ischemic heart disease: prospective evidence from blue-collar men. *Social Science and Medicine*, 31, 1127–34.

Siegrist, J., Peter, R., Motz, W. and Strauer, B. E. (1992). The role of hypertension, left ventricular hypertrophy and psychosocial risks in cardiovascular disease: prospective evidence from blue-collar men. *European Heart Journal*, 13, 89–95.

Skinner, E. A. (1995). Perceived control, motivation and coping. London: Sage.

Sluckin, W., Herbert, M. and Slucking, A. (1983). *Maternal bonding*. Oxford: Blackwell.

Smith, J. A., Harre, R. and Van Langenhove, L. (1995a). *Rethinking methods in psychology*. London: Sage.

Smith, J. A., Harre, R. and Van Langenhove, L. (1995b). *Rethinking psychology*. London: Sage.

Smith, P. B. and Bond, M. H. (1993). *Social psychology across cultures: analysis and perspectives*. London: Harvester/Wheatsheaf.

Smith, T. W. and Anderson, N. B. (1986). Models of personality and disease: an interactional approach to Type A behaviour and cardiovascular risk. *Journal of Personality and Social Psychology*, 50, 1166–73.

Smith, T. and Rhodewalt, F. (1986). On states, traits, and processes: a transactional alternative to the individual difference assumptions in Type A behaviour and physiological reactivity. *Journal of Research in Personality*, 20, 229–51.

Smith, T. W., Pope, M. K., Rhodewalt, F. and Poulton, J. L. (1989). Optimism, neuroticism, coping, and symptom reports: An alternative interpretation of the Life Orientation Test. *Journal of Personality and Social Psychology*, 56, 640–8.

Spiegel, D., Bloom, J., Kraemer, H. and Gotthel, E. (1989). Effect of psychosocial treatment on survival of patients with metastatic breast cancer. *Lancet*, ii, 901.

Spielberger, C. D. (1972). Anxiety as an emotional state. In: C. D. Spielberger (ed.), *Anxiety: current trends in theory and research*. London: Academic Press.

Spielberger, C. D., Gorsuch, R. and Lushene, R. (1970). *The State–Trait Anxiety Inventory (STAI): test manual form X*. Palo Alto, CA: Consulting Psychologists Press.

Spivack, G. and Shure, M. (1974). *Social adjustment of young children: a cognitive approach to solving real-life problems*. San Francisco: Jossey-Bass.

Spruitt, I. P., Bastinaasen, J., Verkley, H. *et al.* (1985). *Experiencing unemployment: financial constraints and health*. Leiden: Institute of Social Medicine.

Stacey, M., Drearden, R., Pill, R. and Robinson, D. (1970). *Hospitals, children and their families: the report of a pilot study*. London: Routledge and Kegan Paul.

Stone, A. A., Cox, D. S., Valdimarsdottir, H. *et al.* (1987a). Evidence that secretory IgA antibody is associated with daily mood. *Journal of Personality and Social Psychology,* 52, 988–93.

Stone, A. A., Reed, B. R. and Neale, J. M. (1987b). Changes in daily event frequency precede episodes of physical symptoms. *Journal of Human Stress,* 13, 70–4.

Stone, A. A., Bovbjerg, D. H., Neale, J. M. *et al.* (1992). Development of the common cold symptoms following experimental rhinovirus infection is related to prior stressful life events. *Behavioural Medicine,* 18, 115–20.

Stone, A. A., Neale, J. M., Cox, D. S. *et al.* (1994). Daily events are associated with a secretory immune response to an oral antigen in men. *Health Psychology,* 13, 440–6.

Stroebe, W., Stroebe, M. S. and Hansson, R. (eds) (1993). *Handbook of bereavement.* New York: Cambridge University Press.

Strongman, K. (1996). *The psychology of emotion,* 4th ed. Chichester: Wiley.

Sweeney, P. D., Anderson, K. and Bailey, S. (1986). Attributional style in depression: a meta-analytic review. *Journal of Personality and Social Psychology,* 50, 974–91.

Syrotuik, J. and D'Arcy, C. (1984). Social support and mental health: direct, protective and compensatory effects. *Social Science and Medicine,* 18, 229–36.

Tajfel, H. and Turner, J. C. (1979). An integrative theory of intergroup conflict. In: S. Worchel and W. G. Austin (eds), *The social psychology of intergroup relations.* Monterey, CA: Brooks-Cole.

Tanwar, S. and Sethi, A. S. (1986). The relationship of sex role orientation, locus of control and achievement motivation to self esteem among college females. *Journal of Psychological Researchers,* 30, 121–8.

Taylor, S. E., Repetti, R. L. and Seeman, T. (1997). Health psychology: what is an unhealthy environment and how does it get under the skin? *Annual Review of Psychology,* 48, 411–47.

Theorell, T., Blomkvist, V., Jonsson, H., Schulman, S., Berntorp, E. and Stigendal, L. (1995). Social support and the development of immune function in human immunodeficiency virus infection. *Psychosomatic Medicine,* 57, 32–6.

Thilagaraj, R. (1984). Achievement motivation of delinquents and non-delinquents. *Social Defence,* 29, 18–20.

Tisdale, D. A. and Lawrence, J. S. (1986). Interpersonal problem-solving competency: review and critique of the literature. *Clinical Psychological Review*, 6, 337–56.

Tizard, B. (1975). Unit autonomy in residential nurseries. In Tizard, J., Sinclair, I. and Clarke, R. (eds), *Varieties of residential experience*. London: Routledge and Kegan Paul.

Tolsdorf, C. (1976). Social networks, support and coping: an exploratory study. *Family Processes*, 15, 407–17.

Turner, J. C. (1985). Social categorisation and the self-concept: a social–cognitive theory of group behaviour. In: E. J. Lawlor (ed.), *Advances in group processes; theory and research*, vol. 2. Greenwich, CT: JAI Press.

Tupes, E. C. and Christal, R. C. (1961) Recurrent personality factors based on trait ratings. Technical Report no. ASDTR/61/97. Lackland Air Force Base, TX: US Air Force.

Ullah, P., Banks, M. and Warr, P. (1985). Social support, social pressures and psychological distress during unemployment. *Psychological Medicine*, 15, 283–95.

Verma, O. P. (1986). Achievement motivation: a multivariate study. *Indian Psychological Review*, 30, 1–3.

Veroff, J. (1982). Assertive motivations: achievement versus power. In: D. G. Winter and A. J. Stewart (eds), *Motivation and society*. San Francisco: Jossey-Bass.

Vogt, T., Mullooly, J., Ernst, D. *et al.* (1992). Social networks as predictors of ischemic heart disease, cancer, stroke and hypertension: Incidence, survival and mortality. *Journal of Clinical Epidemiology*, 45, 659–66.

Warr, P. B. (1978). A study of psychological well-being. *British Journal of Psychology*, 69, 111–21.

Warr, P. B. (1987) *Work, unemployment and mental health*. Oxford: Oxford University Press,

Watson, D. and Pennebaker, J. W. (1989). Health complaints, stress and distress: Exploring the central role of negative affectivity. *Psychological Review*, 96, 234–54.

Weiner, B. (1985). An attributional theory of achievement motivation and emotion. *Psychological Review*, 92, 548–73.

Weiner, B. (1986). *An attributional theory of motivation and emotion*. New York: Springer.

Weiner, B. (1990). Attribution in personality theory. In: L. A. Pervin (ed.), *Handbook of personality: theory and research*. New York: Guildford Press.

Weiner, B., Russell, D. and Lerman, D. (1978). Affective consequences of causal ascriptions. In: J. H. Harvey, W. J. Ickes and R. F. Kidd (eds), *New directions in attribution research*, 2. Hillsdale, NJ: Erlbaum.

Weiner, B., Russell, D. and Lerman, D. (1979). The cognition–emotion process in achievement-related contexts. *Journal of Personality and Social Psychology*, 37, 1211–20.

Weinstein, N. (1984). Why it won't happen to me: perceptions of risk factors and susceptibility. *Health Psychology*, 3, 531–47.

Werner, E. E. (1989). High risk children in young adulthood: a longitudinal study. *American Journal of Orthopsychiatry*, 59, 72–81.

White, D. and Woollett, A. (1992). *Families: a context for development*. London: Falmer Press.

Wirsching, M., Stierlin, H., Hoffman, F. *et al.* (1982). Psychological identification of breast cancer patients before biopsy. *Journal of Psychosomatic Research*, 26, 1–10.

Wrong, D. (1979). *Power: its forms, bases and uses*. Oxford: Blackwell.

Yerkes, R. M. and Dodson, J. D. (1908). The relation of strength of stimulus to rapidity of habit formation. *Journal of Comparative Neurology and Psychology*, 18, 459–82.

Young, L. D. (1992). Psychological factors in rheumatoid arthritis. *Journal of Consulting and Clinical Psychology*, 60, 619–27.

Young, M. and Willmott, P. (1957). *Family and kinship in East London*. London: Routledge and Kegan Paul.

Index